options, we've organized the Parkway's sights
order (south–north), by milepost.

CIVIL WAR AND OTHER MILITARY HISTORY

THE LIVING TRACE

NATIONAL PARK SERVICE (NPS) INFORMATION

(continued on inside back cover)

T0125490

GUIDE TO THE NATCHEZ TRACE PARKWAY

Copyright © 2020 Tim W. Jackson and Taryn Chase Jackson
Copyright © 2005, 2011 F. Lynne Bachleda
All rights reserved
Published by Menasha Ridge Press
Distributed by Publishers Group West
Printed in China
Third edition, third printing 2024

Editor: Ritchey Halphen
Cover design and cartography: Scott McGrew
Photos: Tim W. Jackson and Taryn Chase Jackson, except as noted on-page and as follows: Front cover, Stacie C/ Shutterstock (road), marekuliasz/Shutterstock (bridge inset), and kathrynalaina/Shutterstock (waterfall); back cover, Art Meripol; page x, Drw7116/Shutterstock; pages xii–1, Rita Robinson/Shutterstock; pages 8–9, Melinda Fawver/Shutterstock (lake); pages 28–29, Kara's Photography/Shutterstock (waterfall); pages 46–47, Anton Foltin/ Shutterstock (swamp), F. Lynne Bachleda (inset); pages 58–59, HixnHix/Shutterstock (fences); pages 66–67, traveler jordan/Shutterstock (bridge); pages 134–135: Greiss/Shutterstock
Proofreader: Emily C. Beaumont
Indexer: Galen Schroeder/Dakota Indexing

Library of Congress Cataloging-in-Publication Data

Names: Jackson, Tim W., author. | Jackson, Taryn Chase, author. | Bachleda, F. Lynne, author.

Title: Guide to the Natchez Trace Parkway / Tim W. Jackson and Taryn Chase Jackson, prior edition by F. Lynne Bachleda

Description: Updated and revised, Third edition. | Birmingham : Menasha Ridge Press, 2020. | Includes bibliographical references. | Summary:

"The historical riches, cultural avenues, and exploratory possibilities of the Natchez Trace Parkway are numerous. This park's natural beauty doesn't come from dramatic mountainous overlooks. Instead, you will find mostly flat terrain rendered in a balanced, subtle palette. In the spring, roadside stretches of clover, wildflowers, grassy fields, and dogwood blossoms wave. Summer is often crowned with pure blue skies and a healthy green, divided only by the yellow-striped roadway. In the fall, the soft, gray Spanish moss gives way to the russet of maples and oaks. In winter, the sturdy dark green of mature cedars takes on promising significance." —Provided by publisher.

Identifiers: LCCN 2019029930 (print) | LCCN 2019029931 (ebook) | ISBN 9781634042819 (paperback) | ISBN 9781634042826 (ebook)

Subjects: LCSH: Natchez Trace Parkway—Guidebooks. | Natchez Trace—Guidebooks. | Automobile travel—Natchez Trace Parkway—Guidebooks.

Classification: LCC F217.N37 B33 2020 (print) | LCC F217.N37 (ebook) | DDC 917.62/93504—dc23

LC record available at lccn.loc.gov/2019029930

LC ebook record available at lccn.loc.gov/2019029931

MENASHA RIDGE PRESS

An imprint of AdventureKEEN
2204 First Ave. S., Ste. 102
Birmingham, AL 35233
800-678-7006, fax 877-374-9016

Visit menasharidge.com for a complete listing of our books and for ordering information. Contact us at info@menasharidge.com, facebook.com/menasharidge, or twitter.com/menasharidge with questions or comments. To find out more about who we are and what we're doing, visit blog.menasharidge.com.

All rights reserved. No part of this book may be reproduced in any form, or by any means electronic, mechanical, recording, or otherwise, without written permission from the publisher, except for brief quotations used in reviews.

DISCLAIMER Although Menasha Ridge Press and the authors have made every attempt to ensure that the information in this book is accurate at press time, they are not responsible for any loss, damage, injury, or inconvenience that may occur in the course of using this book.

TABLE OF CONTENTS

Natchez Trace Parkway Map Legend

▬▬▬ Natchez Trace Parkway	31 US highway	MP 375 Milepost marker
▬ ▬ ▬ Historic Route of the Trace	▬ Tennessee Scenic Highway	☆ Trace Top 20 site
65 Interstate highway	48 14 State highway/county road	◇ Natchez Trace beginning/end
▪ Point of interest		

MISSISSIPPI
· · · · · ·
State line

Salem ●
City/town pinpoint

Roosevelt State Park
Park/forest border

River *Lake*
Water feature

🚲 Bike-in-only campground	🛏 Lodging	🚻 Restrooms
⛺ Campground	🚶 Natchez Trace National Scenic Trail	Sanitary disposal station
🥾 Hiking trail	⛱ Picnic area	Self-guided nature trail
🐴 Horse trail	Ranger station	Wheelchair-accessible restrooms

Key to Icons in Text

🚲 Biking	? Information	Ranger station
⛺ Campground	🛏 Lodging	🚻 Restrooms
🍴 Food	⛱ Picnic area	🥾 Trailhead

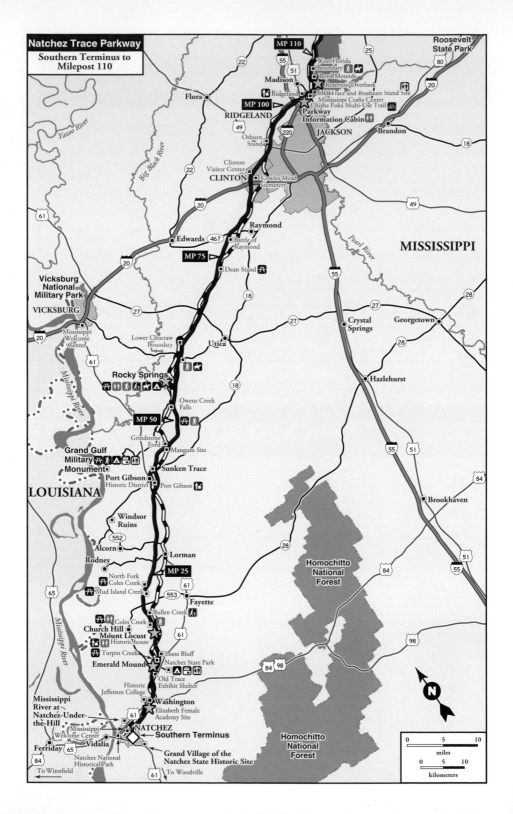

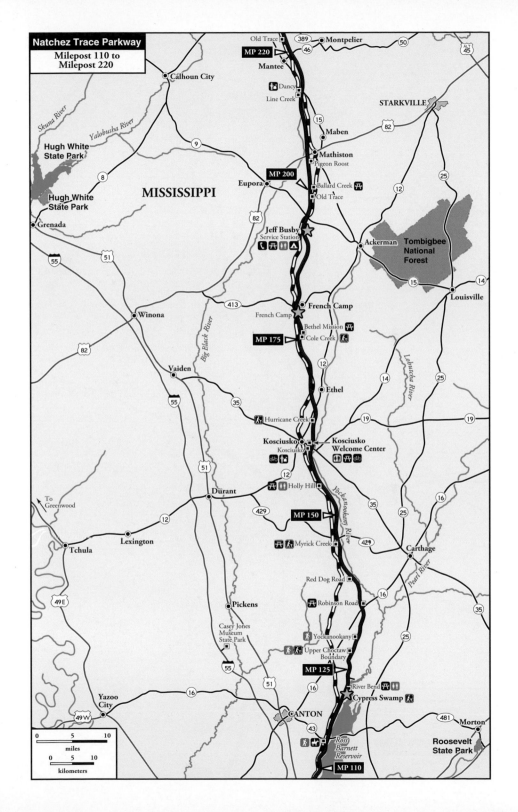

Natchez Trace Parkway
Milepost 110 to
Milepost 220

MISSISSIPPI

STARKVILLE

Old Trace
MP 220
Mantee
Montpelier
Dancy
Line Creek
Cálhoun City
Maben
Mathiston
Pigeon Roost
MP 200
Eupora
Ballard Creek
Old Trace
Hugh White
State Park
Hugh White
State Park
Grenada
Jeff Busby
Service Station
Ackerman
Tombigbee
National
Forest
Louisville
Winona
French Camp
French Camp
Bethel Mission
Cole Creek
MP 175
Vaiden
Ethel
Hurricane Creek
Kosciusko
Kosciusko
Kosciusko
Welcome Center
Durant
Holly Hill
MP 150
To
Greenwood
Myrick Creek
Carthage
Lexington
Tchula
Red Dog Road
Robinson Road
Casey Jones
Museum
State Park
Pickens
Yockanookany
Upper Choctaw
Boundary
MP 125
River Bend
Cypress Swamp
Yazoo
City
CANTON
Ross
Barnett
Reservoir
Roosevelt
State Park
Morton

0   5   10
miles
0   5   10
kilometers

MP 110

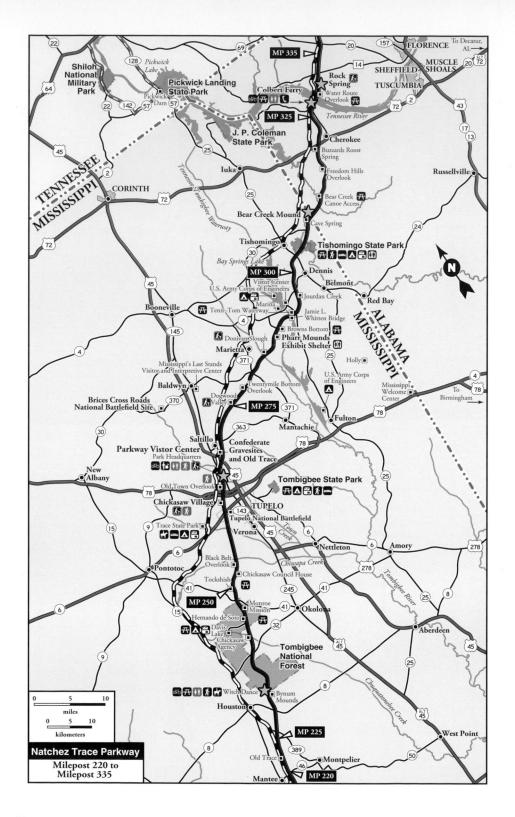

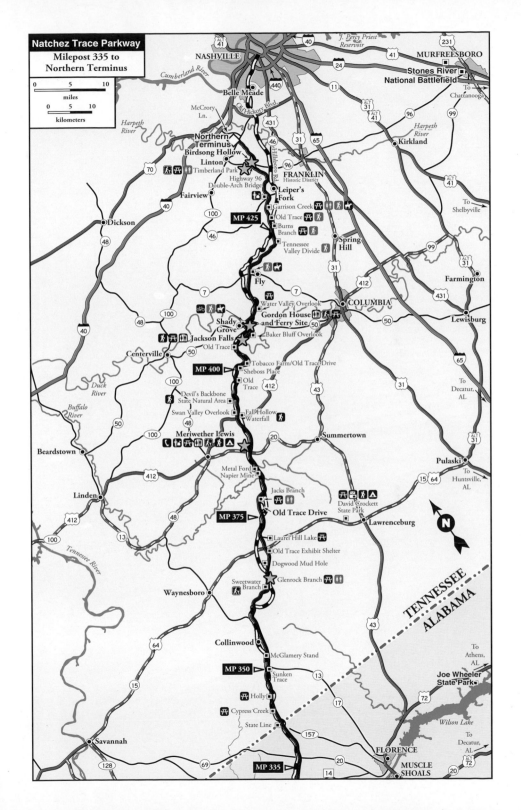

ACKNOWLEDGMENTS

The support of the National Park Service staff at the Natchez Trace Parkway's Tupelo headquarters has been invaluable, and once again they provided crucial updates for the third edition of this book. Our thanks also go to those who have previously written about the Trace and the Parkway (please see Appendix 1, "Information Sources," page 136, for more information).

—Tim W. Jackson and Taryn Chase Jackson

DEDICATION

With gratitude to the Natchez Trace Parkway employees who conserve and maintain this delightful scenic drive and all of its wonders

Introduction

In 1962, when Dr. Dawson Phelps presented himself at the Great Smokies information desk, to the inquiry "Where are you from?" he confessed with some pride to being a Park Service man stationed at the Natchez Trace. To his astonishment the ranger replied, "I certainly feel sorry for you!" To Dr. Phelps's "Why?" the ranger replied, "Because you have nothing for visitors to see."

—John S. Mohlhenrich, former chief park interpreter
for the Trace, in his revision of Dawson Phelps's
Administrative History of the Natchez Trace Parkway (1965)

OVERVIEW

That Smoky Mountains ranger couldn't have been more wrong. Most federal parks or landmarks are devoted to a limited number of themes. The graceful Natchez Trace Parkway "ribbon of time," however, has many threads. It can transport you back 9,000 years to the time of Paleo-Indian hunters, drop you into a Civil War battle, urge you to contemplate "the Nile of the Western Hemisphere," encourage you to empathize with foot-weary 19th-century travelers yearning for home, and teach you about contemporary farming practices. The historical riches, cultural avenues, and exploratory possibilities of the Natchez Trace Parkway are numerous.

This park's natural beauty doesn't come from dramatic mountainous overlooks but instead from mostly flat terrain rendered in a balanced, subtle palette. In the spring, roadside stretches of clover, wildflowers, grassy fields, and dogwood blossoms wave. Summer is often crowned with pure blue skies and a healthy green, divided only by the yellow-striped roadway. In fall the soft gray Spanish moss gives way to the russet of maples and oaks. In winter the sturdy dark green of mature cedars takes on promising significance. The road alternately holds you in the close embrace of its shady refuge or shoots you into light-filled pastures and croplands. This is a hypnotic environment, a soothing melody of forest and field.

The most famous period for this path was from around 1790 to 1820, when it served as one of the primary passageways through the southwest territory of what was then a relatively new country. Farmers, boatmen, diplomats, ladies, preachers, bandits, soldiers, murderers, and slaves used it to travel between Nashville, Tennessee, and Natchez, Mississippi. By 1800 it was also a United States postal route traversed on horseback by courageous men who risked their lives at breakneck speeds. But the Trace has been around for much, much longer than a mere two centuries.

If you're in a hurry, then perhaps you should choose another route: driving at 50 mph is a legal requirement on most stretches, but this slower pace will also help you relax and notice the Parkway's many sights. For those of us enjoying the ride, few things are more irritating than a vehicle riding too close behind, just waiting for an opportunity to zoom past. Also, bikers are often plentiful during warm weather, so it's wise to pay attention and give cyclists the proper amount of space. Using your imagination, you can replicate some of the same experiences that others before you have had here for millennia. After all, many of the vistas have not changed substantially. Ultimately, this is the affirming power of the Trace: along this distance, powerfully strong human and natural links still exist across time.

One of the Natchez Trace Parkway's distinctive entrance signs Photo: F. Lynne Bachleda

WHAT AND WHERE IS THE NATCHEZ TRACE?

The Natchez Trace Parkway is not laid precisely over what the interpretive signs refer to as the Old Trace. In fact, there is no single roadway or course that once composed the Old Trace.

In *The Natchez Trace: Indian Trail to Parkway,* historian Dawson Phelps explains:

> *Historically, there were two, possibly three, Natchez Traces, each having a different origin and purpose. The first was the Indian trail. The second, the so-called Boatman's Trail, was beaten out by men from the Ohio Valley returning to their homes from trading expeditions to Spanish Louisiana. The third was a road which was opened up by the US Government to facilitate overland travel between Natchez and Nashville.*

The modern concept that a road follows a fixed route does not apply to the Natchez Trace. During the short time that the road was a major line of communication, its location shifted to meet the rapidly changing needs of the southwestern frontier. Only rarely do all of the various locations coincide, making it possible to say, "This is the Natchez Trace."

Congress first authorized a survey of the Old Trace for construction of a Natchez Trace Parkway on May 21, 1936. Seventy-one years later—on May 18, 2005—the last section around Jackson, Mississippi, was completed, making the Parkway one seamless journey from Natchez, Mississippi, to Pasquo, Tennessee, about 15 miles southwest of downtown Nashville. The federal lands that border the Parkway average about 412.5 feet on each side of the Parkway, for a total of 52,289 acres.

TOUGH OLD TRACES

This early interstate road-building venture—snake-infested, mosquito-beset, robber-haunted, Indian-traveled forest path—was lamented by the pious, cursed by the impious, and tried everyone's strength and patience.

—National Park Service sign at Sunken Trace, milepost 350.5

Until the 1830s, when the reliability of steamboat travel north on the Mississippi River made it somewhat obsolete, the Natchez Trace was well traveled. This was especially true from about 1790 to 1810.

As you cruise smoothly along the Parkway, imagine setting out to walk north from Natchez nearly 500 miles over twisting, brambly, muddy trails that sometimes disappeared into thick woods or were blocked by large, storm-fallen trees. Having traversed swamps, creeks, and bayous, you still faced the challenge of crossing the Tennessee River and climbing the route's largest ridges. There were critters aplenty, and although danger from the attack of wild animals presented more of a mental hazard than an actual one, 1797 Trace traveler Francis Bailey wrote that he had seen enough wolves, bears, and deer to keep night fires going.

Probably the greatest danger of travel through the wilderness was the possibility of becoming sick or having an injury too severe to reach medical attention on time, if at all. The aggravations didn't have to be life-threatening, however, to make life miserable. Bailey, and no doubt numerous others, suffered from a severe allergy to poison ivy, a plant still abundant today on the Old Trace. His legs were so swollen that he had to make moccasins to replace his snug boots before he could continue his journey. Insects, especially during periods of wet weather, presented another constant discomfort to the travelers.

Petty larceny and horse theft were common occurrences in the Indian country. According to the National Park Service, horse stealing was the most prevalent form of robbery among the natives. The wise traveler anticipating a trip through the wilderness packed iron hobbles to fasten together the legs of his horse so that it could neither stray nor be stolen. Often horses were stolen only to be returned by the thieves a short time later in order to claim a reward.

As if all of these challenges weren't enough, in the early years of the 19th century the Trace came to be plagued by outlaws. Generally very cruel, these mostly white (and some native) bandits and murderers cast a specter of terror over everyone who traveled through the wilderness. Merchants and traders returning from Natchez laden with the profits of their sales made especially easy prey.

The people who survived the walk home proved themselves to be lucky and hardy, to say the least.

THE BIRTH AND DEATH OF THE NATCHEZ TRACE AS A ROAD

This old road, with its distinctive landmarks, forests, canebrakes, ridges, and swamps recalls an early and heroic chapter in our national epic.

—Dawson Phelps, in *An Administrative History of the Natchez Trace Parkway*

The Natchez Trace began as ancient animal trails worn by creatures heading toward the salt springs in what is now Nashville, Tennessee. The passage and its parts were variously called the Chickasaw Trail, Path to the Choctaw Nation, Boatman's Trail, Natchez Road, Nashville Road, Mail Road, and even Cumberland Road. It became known as the Natchez Trace sometime after its heavy use dwindled in the 1820s.

The Trace passes through lands that the Natchez, Choctaw, and Chickasaw Nations used primarily for dwelling, farming, and hunting. Hernando de Soto claimed this territory for Spain in 1540–41. By 1798 Spain had relinquished its claims north of the 31st parallel, which cuts across the Deep South in southern Mississippi; this freed the port of Natchez to open more widely to Mississippi River trade. The influx of boatmen who needed a way home did much to publicize the route.

As commerce and land attracted more settlers, the US government needed a quicker way to communicate with the Mississippi Territory, so in 1800 it established the postal route between Nashville and Natchez. Indian treaties permitted the establishment of a road, and in 1801 the project began under the command of the notorious General James Wilkinson.

In 1806 Congress appropriated $6,000 to improve the road, probably to mollify the complaints of postal riders. No maintenance money was provided, however, and to the dismay of its many travelers, the road soon returned to its rugged form.

Military use of the route peaked during the war years of 1812–15, when Andrew Jackson traveled the Trace with his men. After his victory at the Battle of New Orleans, military needs for the road ceased, and so did much congressional interest in it.

Still, the postal riders continued their brave journeys along the old road, and by 1816 there were three mail deliveries a week. The government began to rely more on the steamboat to carry the mail in the 1820s.

THE RESURRECTION OF THE NATCHEZ TRACE AS A PARKWAY

It requires no stretch of the imagination to look back upon a time when the Natchez Trace was practically unknown to the people of Mississippi. . . . But with pardonable pride, we claim for the Mississippi Society of the Daughters of the American Revolution [DAR] the credit for awakening general public interest.

—Mrs. A. F. Fox of West Point, Mississippi, 1910

After about 85 years of disuse, the rebirth of the Trace likely started with a 1905 article by John Swain titled "The Natchez Trace" that appeared in *Everybody's Magazine.* That same year Mrs. Egbert Jones, a member of the Holly Springs, Mississippi, chapter of the DAR, proposed that the DAR commemorate the Trace by placing an interpretive marker in every county through which the Trace ran; DAR chapters in Tennessee and Alabama were enlisted to aid the Mississippi chapters' efforts. The LaSalle chapter placed a monument in Tishomingo in 1908, and the Mississippi statewide chapter placed one overlooking the Mississippi River at Natchez in 1909.

When the lure of history failed to ignite more public interest in the Trace's preservation, the DAR changed tactics toward the public's desire for good roads. The Pave the Trace campaign, formally inaugurated in 1916 by the Natchez Chamber of Commerce, was short-lived, but it was a start.

A turning point for the Trace occurred in March 1933, when Thomas L. Bailey, a Mississippi state legislator who went on to be elected governor in 1943, delivered an address at a DAR marker dedication in the town of Mathiston in Webster County. This caught the attention of Ned Lee, editor of the *Webster Progress* newspaper, who assigned columnist Jim Walton to research and write about the Trace in his "Nits and Tidbits" column. In August 1933 Walton suggested to Mississippi Congressman Jeff Busby that he introduce a bill in Congress to survey the Old Trace.

The timing was right, as the country was looking for New Deal projects that would benefit the public, stimulate economically depressed areas, and provide work for people in desperate need of a job during the Great Depression. The National Recovery Act of 1933 called for a comprehensive system of public works that included highways and parkways.

Backed by much local support, Busby introduced two bills in the US House of Representatives. The first would authorize $50,000 to survey the Old Trace, and the second asked for $25 million to construct the Natchez Trace Parkway. Only the survey money was approved at that time, but on June 30, 1937, construction finally began when three grading permits were issued in Mississippi.

On May 18, 1938, the Natchez Trace Parkway, which still had miles and miles to go, was created as a unit of the National Park Service (NPS). Federal funding came in fits and starts over the next 60-plus years. May 21, 2005, marked the conclusion of piecemeal road construction when the segment around Jackson was opened with great fanfare. The Natchez Trace Parkway's legacy continues, however, with the acquisition of new interpretive sites and plans for additional visitor centers.

HOW TO USE THIS GUIDE

The core of this book is Chapter 5, "Sightseeing by Milepost" (page 66). It's organized to correspond to the NPS's Natchez Trace map and brochure, which is widely available at Parkway visitor centers (see page 26) and online at nps.gov /natr/planyourvisit/maps.htm. The maps in this book, adapted from the NPS map, are found on pages vi–ix.

The milepost system, explained in Chapter 2, "The Nuts and Bolts of Traveling the Trace" (page 28), correlates the various sights with the Parkway's roadside markers running numerically from south to north. This was the direction in which the Trace was most often traveled during its busiest years.

"Sightseeing by Milepost" is also broken down by cities and states—the geographical touchstones with which people are most familiar. With only a few exceptions, all of the stops in this book are on the map. We encourage you to explore places that pertain to the Trace story—for example, downtown Nashville's Tennessee Bicentennial Capitol Mall, where ancient animals that once trod the Trace's paths gathered at the sulfur salt spring.

The Appendixes (starting on page 134) list information sources that can help you find what you want to see along the Trace, along with our recommendations for places to stay along the way. We've made every effort to provide you with as much information as possible to help you plan your trip.

Enjoy your travels on the Trace. It is a truly special place that willingly reveals itself to you if you meet it with an expansive imagination and the gift of your time.

CHAPTER 1
Traveling Your Own Trace

> You have lots of options for exploring the Parkway.
> This chapter helps you sort them out.

"SHOULD WE STOP HERE?"

T his is probably the most commonly asked question on the Natchez Trace
Parkway. There are about 100 possible milepost stops, so you have a lot of
options: exploring a 200-year-old log cabin, studying a swamp, climbing
a prehistoric people's ceremonial mound, enjoying a roadside picnic, hiking an
ancient animal path, and visiting the place where Elvis was born are each possibilities in a single day of travel along the Parkway.

To help you sort out your options, we've created categories to help key you in;
for convenience, we also list these categories on the inside front and back covers.

PARKWAY CATEGORIES

The most important category is the **Trace Top 20.** These are the sights that we
don't want you to miss—they represent the best of what the Parkway has to offer.
Each is marked on the maps with a star (✪).

The Trace Top 20

In an update from the previous edition of this book, we decided (with one excep-
tion) to limit the Trace Top 20 to sites that are actually on the Parkway—a few
great sites have fallen off the list because we decided they simply represented too
far of a detour. That said, if you have the time to work in some side trips, you
should definitely try to see **Brices Cross Roads National Battlefield** (milepost
266.0), **Vicksburg National Military Park** (milepost 38.0), and the **Windsor
Ruins** (mileposts 30.0 and 41.0).

The one site in this edition's Trace Top 20 that isn't directly on the Parkway is
Emerald Mound, which is only about a mile off the route and is remarkable in size.

This category naturally has a bit of everything in it—a testament to the Parkway's variety. We've listed them in ascending milepost order, south–north, for easy
reference. Each is marked on the maps with a star (✪). Within Chapter 5, "Sightseeing by Milepost" (page 66), you can find more information on each of these
highly recommended stops. Note, too, that the Parkway starts on the edge of

Natchez and goes through Jackson and Tupelo. All three Mississippi cities have lots to do and an abundance of restaurants and accommodations.

1. **ELIZABETH FEMALE ACADEMY** (milepost 5.1, page 74) This school for women opened in late 1818 in the community of Washington, just a few miles outside of Natchez, and closed in 1845. Not much is left behind, but a 2- to 3-minute walk on a paved path takes you to the ruins, which are remarkable due to their age and history: the academy was the first degree-granting institution for women chartered in the very new state of Mississippi. John James Audubon once taught here.

2. **EMERALD MOUND** (milepost 10.3, page 76) Remarkably underrated, this is the second largest Mississippian mound in the United States and is designated as a National Historic Landmark. You do have to exit the Parkway to get there, but it's only about a mile away on a rough country road and covers about 8 acres. It is estimated that construction on the main platform began around AD 1350. The site was abandoned by the late 1600s, when a new capital for the Natchez Indians was built at the Grand Village in Natchez.

3. **MOUNT LOCUST HISTORIC INN AND PLANTATION** (milepost 15.5, page 78) The Mount Locust Inn is one of the oldest buildings in Mississippi and the only pre-1820 hostelry that remains along the Parkway. Built in 1780, it was quite popular during the era of foot and horse travel along the Trace and has been restored to reflect the period. With restrooms and an interpretive center, Mount Locust makes an excellent stop for a picnic and some history.

4. **ROCKY SPRINGS** (milepost 54.8, page 84) This stop is truly one of our favorites. It offers a campground and is the site of a village established in 1790, though all that remains is a couple of rusty bank safes, a church, and a cemetery. A walk through the cemetery makes one think of the hardscrabble life of the residents of Rocky Springs who endured Union occupation, yellow fever, boll weevils, and finally the death of the springs itself.

5. **PARKWAY INFORMATION CABIN AND CHISHA FOKA MULTI-USE TRAIL** (milepost 102.4, page 88) Cyclists, joggers, and walkers will love this 10-mile trail, which extends east–west from the site of the 19th-century Choctaw Agency (milepost 100.7, page 87) to the Ross R. Barnett Reservoir Overlook (see page 88). The trail passes the Parkway Information Cabin, which is a great place for, well, information, but also for a bathroom break. The creation of this trail earned the Jackson suburb of Ridgeland, Mississippi, a Bicycle Friendly Community designation from the League of American Bicyclists.

6. **ROSS R. BARNETT RESERVOIR OVERLOOK** (milepost 105.6, page 88) If you enjoy chilling out near a big body of water, here's your only chance to do so along the Parkway. The reservoir covers 33,000 acres, and you'll drive alongside it for roughly 8 miles. The overlook offers you an opportunity to stop and soak in the views. It's a great spot for a picnic or to launch a run or bike ride along the Chisha Foka Multi-Use Trail (see 49).

7. **CYPRESS SWAMP** (milepost 122.0, page 90) Less than 0.5 mile long, the Cypress Swamp Loop Trail can be easily hiked in 20 minutes. If you've envisioned a Deep South with Spanish moss swaying in a slight breeze over swampy marshes where alligators prowl, this is where your dreams meet reality.

8. **FRENCH CAMP HISTORIC VILLAGE** (milepost 180.7, page 94) In this re-created pre–Civil War log-cabin village, you'll find a gift shop, bed-and-breakfast, museum, carriage house, blacksmith shop, church, and the Col. James Drane House (1846). Expanded and updated in 2019, the Council House Café (see page 94) is the only restaurant within sight of the Parkway in all of Mississippi.

9. **JEFF BUSBY PARK** (milepost 193.1, page 95) With more than 20 picnic tables and at least half that many grills, this a wonderful spot for a picnic and also one of the best camping sites along the Parkway. You can stretch your legs on the Little Mountain Trail or the nature trail. If you make it to the Little Mountain Exhibit and Overlook on a clear day, you have a view of about 20 miles.

10. **WITCH DANCE** (milepost 233.2, page 98) A top spot for equestrians and hikers, Witch Dance has an 18-mile dual-use trail that is considered one of the top horse trails in Mississippi. Restrooms, hitching posts, parking, picnic tables, and grills are all provided, so you can spend a whole day here if you want.

11. **PARKWAY VISITOR CENTER AND HEADQUARTERS** (milepost 266.0, page 103) This is *the* place to go for information about the Parkway, but it offers much more: interpretive exhibits, a video presentation, a bookstore and gift shop, and wonderful NPS staff to help you make the most of your Natchez Trace trip. While you're here, stretch your legs on the paved nature walk.

12. **BEAR CREEK MOUND** (milepost 308.8, page 108) Bear Creek Mound is among the oldest Indian mounds on the Parkway. When you stand here, you're amid the shadows of people who used the adjacent village site 9,000 years ago. A creek is an easy walk from the mound and a shady spot to visit.

13. **COLBERT FERRY** (milepost 327.3, page 111) The ferry itself is long gone, but this is an excellent riverside recreation area with a boat ramp, picnic tables and grills, restrooms, and lovely river views. Bring your swimsuit and spend the afternoon.

14. **ROCK SPRING** (milepost 330.2, page 116) A jewel of a nature retreat that fol-lows a crystal-clear spring back to its source.

15. **GLENROCK BRANCH** (milepost 364.5, page 118) This place is just cool, figura-tively and literally. With lots of shade and a broad creek running through, it's a wonderful warm-weather spot for splashing around or enjoying a picnic. From the parking lot and restrooms, a quick jaunt into this natural amphitheater allows you to explore the limestone rock formations in a lovely natural setting in the bend of the aforementioned creek.

16. MERIWETHER LEWIS PARK AND NATIONAL MONUMENT (milepost 385.9, page 120) Visit the gravesite of one of America's most promising young heroes, he of Lewis and Clark fame. While there's some debate regarding whether Lewis was murdered or committed suicide here on the Trace, the likelihood of the latter is high. This stop offers camping, a pioneer cemetery, and lots of room to roam.

17. JACKSON FALLS (milepost 404.7, page 125) A short but mildly challenging hike here will reward you with the sight of refreshing falls rippling down a high limestone bank. The Baker Bluff Overlook offers vistas of a broad field in the distance. Restrooms, picnic tables, and grills make this a good stop even if you don't hike to the falls.

18. GORDON HOUSE AND FERRY SITE (milepost 407.7, page 127) One of only two original Trace-era structures that are still standing, this is the nearly 200-year-old home of John and Dolly Gordon. Dolly managed a 1,500-acre plantation, raised 10 children, and lived here for 40 years after John died. Restrooms and picnic tables make this a convenient rest stop—or, for those who prefer to stretch their legs, a brief hike to the probable site of the ferry service that John Gordon founded to cross the Duck River.

During summer, visitors use this spot as a natural slide at Jackson Falls.

19. TIMBERLAND PARK (milepost 437.2, page 130) A great addition to the wondrous stops along the Parkway, Timberland Park opened in 2014. Operated by Williamson County (Tennessee) Parks & Recreation, it's just a few miles from the Parkway's northern terminus. Among its offerings are an interpretive center, a butterfly garden, hiking trails, picnic tables, an overlook, and restrooms. It's also open to RVs and has an ADA-accessible trail.

20. BIRDSONG HOLLOW (milepost 438.0, page 131) A soaring double-arch bridge spans a quiet valley in this breakthrough feat of engineering that has won numerous design awards. Enjoy the view from the top or down in the valley.

Other Categories

- The Old Trace
- Kaintuck Boatmen and the Postal Road
- Archaeology and American Indians
- Natural Wonders
- Civil War and Other Military History
- The Living Trace
- National Park Service (NPS) Information

The following descriptions will give you a context and understanding for each Trace category.

THE OLD TRACE

> *We got safe across [the Duck River]. On the opposite shore we found it difficult to rejoin the path which led to our destined port, as there were so many paths crossing and recrossing each other.*
>
> —Francis Bailey, Trace traveler in 1797
> and author of *Early Travels in the Tennessee Country*

The historical route of the Old Trace, which only sometimes runs concurrently with the modern Parkway, was never a single path running from Natchez to Nashville. These natural trails attracted centuries of American Indians in search of game. In time, the Trace became a meandering mishmash that was often obscured by the effects of weather.

More than 120 years passed between the heyday of the Trace as a foot-and-bridle path, around 1810, and the Congressionally authorized survey to reclaim it.

You have several opportunities to walk or drive parts of the Old Trace. Most sections are short and take only 5–10 minutes to explore. One of the more visually romantic sections, the so-called **Sunken Trace,** is at milepost 41.5. At mileposts 198.6 and 221.4, the Old Trace crosses the Parkway, so you get a first-hand look at the meandering quality of the original route. At milepost 350.5 you can discern where the road was rerouted to avoid mud holes. Drivers (except those pulling trailers) can enjoy a 2.5-mile driving section starting at milepost 375.8. The Old Trace stop at milepost 397.4 permits you to walk 2 miles to the **Garrison Creek** pull-off. One of the longer sections is at milepost 403.7, where the path is about 0.6 mile out-and-back.

Trace Tip

When you take note of what is marked on the NPS map of the Natchez Trace Parkway as the "historic route of the Trace," understand that in many cases you're looking at an approximation.

There is no substitute for experiencing all of the Old Trace that you can.

KAINTUCK BOATMEN AND THE POSTAL ROAD

Bands of travelers moved closer together, with intenser caution, through the glassy tunnels of the Trace, for all the proportion went away, and they followed one another like insects going at dawn through the heavy grass.

—Eudora Welty, "First Love"

Traffic on the Mississippi River transformed the Natchez Trace into one of America's most important historic roads. As increasing numbers of settlers pushed into the Ohio River Valley in the late 1700s, they began to look to the Mississippi and Ohio Rivers to get their goods to market. Using flatboats and sometimes keelboats, these farmers became part-time boatmen.

Floating downstream was precarious, but pulling or rowing a boat upstream was even more difficult and dangerous. Eventually, boatmen who stopped at Natchez learned of an overland route through Indian territory back to Nashville, where they could head home by a less arduous and risky path. Kentuckians were particularly prominent among the men who floated downstream on the Cumberland, Tennessee, Ohio, and Mississippi Rivers, and then sold their goods—including their boats, for lumber—at Natchez before they began the walk home. Thus, the whole group became known as Kaintucks, regardless of their states of origin.

The approximate distance between Natchez and Nashville was estimated at more than 500 miles, and the time required to travel the distance varied considerably. In rare instances, travel on horseback between Natchez and Nashville could be accomplished in 10–12 days, although under normal circumstances approximately 20 days were required. For those traveling on foot, an average of 25 miles per day was feasible, and the trip might thus take approximately 20–30 days. Today, of course, you can travel between Natchez and Nashville in one day.

As the southwestern frontier territory became more populated, Washington, DC, bureaucrats developed a need to communicate with the people living there. So as boatmen were tramping home, mail began moving along the Trace. With all this traffic rose the need for lodging. In 1801 the Choctaws and the Chickasaws agreed to permit inns on their lands. Typically these inns, or "stands," had some connection to the Indian tribes if they were on Indian land. Sheboss Place in Chickasaw country, for example, was owned by a native man and his white wife.

Trace Tip

Most of the Trace's primitive, often hastily built stands (inns) are long gone, but the NPS has managed to protect many of the sites where they were located. Mount Locust (see page 78), for example, is home to a surviving circa-1780 inn and plantation house.

In more cases than not, the meals offered at stands consisted of only a mess of mush and milk, some fried bacon, and possibly some fresh meat. Sleeping arrangements generally consisted of the hard floor of the one-room structure, although travelers always had the option of sleeping outside. Charges for these services varied from 10¢ to 25¢ per person.

These stands, which at one time numbered more than 50, were mostly crude, one-room shelters but were welcome sights to Trace-weary travelers.

Post riders had to endure all the difficulties of the Trace under the added duress of a tight schedule, which sometimes required that they even ride at night with little regard for personal safety. Groups of travelers tried to band together, keeping to the "safety in numbers" adage. Moving in a group could be extraordinarily slow, however, so a few struck out on their own, praying that nothing deadly would befall them. Oftentimes they were not so fortunate.

Until about 1803, when the federal government began to crack down on their activities, bandits were a real problem on the Trace. If solo travelers, who were known to be carrying profits from sales in Natchez and New Orleans, went alone into the wild territory of the Trace, they were often met with mayhem.

During the 40 years between 1790 and 1830, the Natchez Trace carried many thousands of homeward-bound boatmen as well as an assortment of other travelers, such as slave traders headed south to Forks at the Road, one of the largest slave markets in the United States. With the appearance of steamboats during the mid-1810s, foot travel over the Trace began to slowly decline. New federal roads, such as the Jackson Military Road that shaved 200 miles off the distance between Nashville and New Orleans, also lessened traffic on the Trace.

Kaintuck Boatmen and the Postal Road

— *	The Mississippi River at Natchez-Under-the-Hill (p. 71)
15.5	Mount Locust Historic Inn and Plantation (p. 78)
45.7	Grindstone Ford and Mangum Mound (p. 83)
73.5	Dean Stand (p. 86)
93.1	Osburn Stand (p. 87)
104.5	Old Trace and Brashears Stand Site (p. 88)
135.5	Robinson Road (p. 91)
180.7	French Camp Historic Village (p. 94)
203.5	Pigeon Roost (p. 96)
249.6	Tockshish (p. 99)
327.3	Colbert Ferry (p. 111)
352.9	McGlamery Stand (p. 117)
382.8	Metal Ford (p. 120)
400.2	Sheboss Place (p. 124)
407.7	Gordon House and Ferry Site (p. 127)

*Indicates that the point of interest is located before the official start of the Natchez Trace Parkway.

ARCHAEOLOGY AND AMERICAN INDIANS

For more than a century the ghosts of a vanished nation have ambuscaded in the vast solitudes of the continent, and the forest-covered mounds have been usually regarded as the mysterious sepulchers of its kings and nobles. It was an alluring conjecture that a powerful people . . . once occupied the valley.

—J. W. Powell, Bureau of American Ethnology, 1891

If you're fascinated by ancient sites and eager to know more about the Indians of the Mississippi River Valley, you'll find the Parkway a chain of historical delights. The sites in Natchez and along the roadway span 9,000 years, three ancient cultures, and three modern tribes.

PREHISTORIC SITES All seven mound locations within Parkway boundaries are in Mississippi; five are burial mounds and two are ceremonial. Burial mounds are usually conical or rounded, and ceremonial mounds are generally flat-topped to accommodate a religious structure, such as a temple. Please respect the mounds.

The architects of the flat-top structures are called Mississippian Mound Build-ers—a name that refers not to the state of Mississippi but to the concentration of the builders' dwellings and villages in the Mississippi River Valley. Although some-times lacking precise links, historians think that these people were the ancestors of the modern, or so-called historic tribes. Along the Parkway these include the Nat-chez, the Choctaw, and the Chickasaw, who all spoke Muskogean languages.

A tie has been established between the Mississippians who built the breath-taking **Emerald Mound** and the Natchez tribe, who abandoned it and subse-quently constructed **Grand Village** as their ceremonial center. When Spanish explorer Hernando de Soto visited the area in 1540, the flat-top mounds were in use, but only the Natchez were still using them when the French arrived 160 years later. Internal strife, diseases introduced by de Soto's men, and conflicts with other tribes gradually took their toll on the tribespeople's daily lives, and over time the flat-top mounds were largely abandoned by the Natchez.

Moving backward in time, several burial sites on the Parkway, including the **Boyd, Bynum,** and **Pharr Mounds,** were inhabited by Woodland Period Indians. They developed a primitive agricultural society and discovered that hunting was more efficient with the bow and arrow. They were also the first to domesticate corn.

Bear Creek Mound and the adjacent area, situated just below the Alabama state line, is one of the oldest occupied sites on the Parkway. This area was inter-mittently inhabited by humans for approximately 8,000 years, first by Paleo-Indians from as early as AD 7000 to Mississippian-era people around AD 1300. The Mississippians built this mound between AD 1200 and 1400 in several stages for ceremonial or possibly elite residential use.

Prehistoric Sites

THE NATCHEZ Until they were defeated and dispersed by the French in the early 1700s, the Natchez Nation was a historical link between ancient and modern American Indian cultures. They had a closely knit society that depended on agri-culture, fishing, and hunting, and they used tools made of stone, wood, and bone until trade with white explorers and pioneers gave them access to iron and steel.

They lived in the vicinity of present-day Natchez, and their ceremonial mounds still stand at **Grand Village** (see page 73).

Built upon mounds 8–10 feet high, Natchez temples were rectangular, measured up to 20 by 40 feet, and were oriented to the east. A bird effigy carved of wood rested upon the gabled roof ends. In a larger front room burned the eternal fire. The back of the building was a small, partitioned holy room where a stone idol or sacred stone was probably kept, and fine mats decorated the walls.

Their supreme deity was the sun. The high priest, called a Sun, was the earthly representative of the deity and was considered a descendant of it. The Sun wielded absolute power of life and death over his subjects. There were male and female Suns, with matriarchal lineage.

As noted earlier, Mississippian Indian ancestors of the Natchez may also have built **Emerald Mound** (see page 76).

Very few Natchez still live in Mississippi. After the tribe was disbanded by the French in the aftermath of the Natchez War in 1730, many Natchez were sold into slavery in the Caribbean; others fled Mississippi and found refuge with other tribes across the South. Today many Natchez are affiliated with the Cherokee, Muscogee (Creek), Seminole, and Sac and Fox Nations of Oklahoma. In South Carolina, the state-recognized **Edisto Natchez–Kusso Tribe** and **Eastern Band Natchez** are the descendants of Mississippi Natchez refugees. The **Natchez Nation** (natcheznation.com), based in Oklahoma, works to preserve tribal ties among today's scattered Natchez communities.

The Natchez

10.3   Emerald Mound (p. 76)

THE CHOCTAW This tribe had the Southeast's best farmers, growing plenty of food to feed themselves with enough left over to barter. The tribe has only one surviving earthwork: the sacred mound of **Nanih Waiya,** near present-day Noxapater, Mississippi (about 30 miles east of the Parkway near Kosciusko). One of the more important surviving American Indian sites in the state, it could be described as the Mecca of Choctaw life and death.

Glimpses of Choctaw life along the Parkway emphasize tribal boundaries that moved several times to accommodate pioneer settlement. The 1820 Treaty of Doaks Stand was an important agreement between the US government and the native peoples living in the Mississippi–Alabama area. Negotiations between whites and Indians were set in writing in treaties, sometimes under threat of coercion from government leaders such as Andrew Jackson. You can also find evidence of the peaceful coexistence between the Choctaw and the new settlers in the stands, or inns, they operated together, often as married couples. Pioneer mission schools point to a more aggressive white imposition of Old World culture on the area's indigenous peoples.

Unlike the Chickasaw (see next section) and the Natchez (see previous section), today's Choctaw maintain a significant presence in Mississippi as well as Oklahoma. The **Mississippi Band of Choctaw Indians** (www.choctaw.org), comprising eight federally recognized communities in 10 counties, operates several cultural–historical sites in addition to Pearl River Resort, a hotel and casino. (For information on the Choctaw Nation in Oklahoma, visit choctawnation.com.)

The Choctaw

61.0	Lower Choctaw Boundary (p. 86)
100.7	Choctaw Agency (p. 87)
128.4	Upper Choctaw Boundary (p. 91)
140.0	Red Dog Road (p. 91)
176.3	Bethel Mission (p. 93)
213.3	Line Creek (p. 97)

Tishomingo State Park (milepost 304.5, page 108) is named for a Chickasaw chief.
Photo: Jason Patrick Ross/Shutterstock

THE CHICKASAW A highly respected nation, the Chickasaw were by far the most warlike tribe in Mississippi, fighting as far north as the Great Lakes and as far south as the Gulf of Mexico. They sometimes fought alone; at times they allied with other Indian nations, and they had a perpetual partnership with the English. Ackia (pronounced "Hehkia"), near Tupelo, was the site of one of their most famous battles. Here, with some English aid, they defeated encroaching Choctaw and French forces. This definitive battle, on May 26, 1736, marked the beginning of the decline of the French presence west of the Appalachian Mountains.

Two stops along the Parkway address the coming together of white and native peoples at US government outposts for Indian relations known as *agencies:* the former site of an inn at **Buzzard Roost Spring** and **Monroe Mission.** At these sites you can learn about Chickasaw daily life, government, and dwellings. **Tishomingo State Park,** named for the last great warrior chief of the Chickasaw Nation, is particularly beautiful. In 1838 Tishomingo died at age 102 on the Trail of Tears and was buried near Little Rock. As the heart of the tribe, Tishomingo is represented on the Great Seal of the Chickasaw Nation, which today is based in Oklahoma (visit chickasaw.net for more information).

The Chickasaw

CIVIL WAR AND OTHER MILITARY HISTORY

Gentle winds of Springtime seem a sighing over a thousand new-made graves.

—A Union soldier who survived the Battle of Shiloh

In the way we think of uniformed soldiers, the first military presence along the Trace was that of Hernando de Soto and his men, although certainly American Indians had organized fighting forces here long before de Soto's men arrived in 1540–41. In 1801–02 the US Army was stationed at the northern end of Garrison Creek with the task of transforming the Old Trace into a more reliable road. In 1813 Andrew Jackson marched troops on the Trace for the War of 1812, and then in 1815 marched his men home again after defeating the British at the Battle of New Orleans.

Two Civil War sites are located directly on the Parkway: the site of the **Battle of Raymond** and a number of **Confederate gravesites.** The adjacent area also has rich stories to tell about the Civil War era, and you may want to venture off the Parkway to visit **Vicksburg, Tupelo, Brices Cross Roads,** and **Shiloh National Battlefields and Military Parks.**

"We must this day conquer or perish!" was Albert Sidney Johnston's prophetic sentiment on the morning of April 6, 1862, at Shiloh in Tennessee. By 2:30 that afternoon, the Confederate commander was dead. This first major battle in the West, also known as Pittsburg Landing, was the bloodiest since the war began in 1861. After two days of fighting, nearly 24,000 men had been killed, wounded, or captured. This Confederate loss was the first in a chain of defeats, and by the evening of June 6, 1862, the western two-thirds of Tennessee was in Union hands.

Traveling to Vicksburg will make evident the Mississippi River's strategic importance in the Union's war efforts. The siege of Vicksburg, "The Gibraltar of the Confederacy," lasted from May 18 to July 4, 1863, subjecting the civilian population to regular shelling and deep deprivation. The loss of Vicksburg, along with Confederate failures at the Battle of Raymond and Port Gibson, inserted a fatal Union wedge into the Confederate States of America (CSA). When Port Hudson, Louisiana, surrendered on July 8, 1863, the North gained complete control of the vital Mississippi River.

In a related but geographically separate effort, Union troops fought to cut through the Confederacy from northern Mississippi to the Atlantic Ocean at Savannah. You can learn more about this struggle, including the battles of Tupelo and Brices Cross Roads, by diverging off the Parkway. Both clashes involved CSA General Nathan Bedford Forrest, whose goal was to interrupt the Union's ability to supply General William Tecumseh Sherman's infamous March to the Sea.

While the battle of Brices Cross Roads, fought on June 10, 1864, was an overwhelming Confederate victory over a larger and better-equipped Union army, the Battle of Tupelo on July 14–15, 1864, is regarded as either a Union victory or a draw. Both battles prevented Forrest from interrupting Sherman's railroad supply line through Louisville, Nashville, and Chattanooga. Both battlefield sites are commemorated by 1-acre plots, and Brices Cross Roads has a museum.

Civil War and Other Military History

38.0	Vicksburg National Military Park (p. 80)
78.3	Battle of Raymond (p. 86)
243.3	Hernando de Soto (p. 98)
259.7	Tupelo National Battlefield (p. 102)
266.0	Brices Cross Roads National Battlefield Site (p. 104)
269.4	Old Trace and Confederate Gravesites (p. 105)
320.3	Shiloh National Military Park (p. 110)
427.6	Garrison Creek (p. 129)

NATURAL WONDERS

A long park has replaced a wild forest.

—Paul R. Coppock, *Memphis Commercial Appeal,* December 26, 1976

In some ways the Parkway is one great outdoor museum, so it follows that many stops give you a chance to examine the Parkway's diverse natural features. Quite a few are simple, scenic picnic areas, while others have NPS interpretations that specifically address the surrounding flora and fauna. Almost all of the nature walks are very short (about 10–15 minutes) and pretty easy to maneuver.

Within the park, more than 2,200 plants help support more than 350 animal species, including a few that are quite rare. Look carefully and you may glimpse the Southern bald eagle, the red-cockaded woodpecker, and the gray bat—all endangered. The area's bayou darter, slackwater darter, and ringed sawback turtle are also on the threatened list. Some of the more common wildlife along the entire length of the Parkway includes white-tailed deer, turkey, bobcat, raccoon, opossum, fox, coyote, and field- and forest-dwelling songbirds. See Chapter 2, "The Nuts and Bolts of Traveling the Trace" (page 28), for more information on potentially dangerous species you might encounter.

See Chapter 2, "The Nuts and Bolts of Traveling the Trace" (page 28),

> ## Trace Tip
>
> From Natchez, Mississippi, to near Nashville, Tennessee, the Parkway cuts through six major forest types and eight major watersheds. The park ranges from 70 to 1,100 feet in elevation, resulting in a variety of habitats.

Natchez, the southern terminus of the Natchez Trace Parkway, is located on a bluff 100 feet above the Mississippi River—definitely a sight worth seeing. From here the Parkway winds northeast through beech and oak forests, with some trees draped with Spanish moss. It enters the Southern Pine Hills near Raymond, Mississippi, and passes through the Jackson Prairie, now occupied by the Jackson metropolitan area and the Ross R. Barnett Reservoir.

From the northeastern tip of the reservoir, the Parkway crosses pine and dry-oak forests in Mississippi's North Central Hills, Flatwoods, and Pontotoc Ridge provinces. European settlers leased large parts of these woodland areas to plant cotton in the red clay soil. This gave rise to the region's antebellum society. The plantations have long since vanished, but agriculture remains important in this part of the state.

The alluvial agricultural soils around Tupelo are part of the Black Belt Prairie and were an important resource to the Chickasaw and the prehistoric Indians who preceded them. North of Tupelo, the Parkway cuts through a mixture of pine and hardwood forests in the hills above the Tombigbee River. The Parkway then makes its way up onto Alabama's Cumberland Plateau, the westernmost extension of the legendary Appalachian Mountain range.

The Parkway drops from the plateau into the Tennessee River Valley of northeastern Alabama with its red clay soils, excellent for growing cotton. It then traverses forests dominated primarily by oak and hickory on Tennessee's Highland Rim, where the road curves more as it reaches its highest elevation of 1,100 feet above sea level. The Parkway terminus at Pasquo, Tennessee, 15 miles outside of Nashville proper, is on the eastern edge of the Nashville Basin, an area similar to the Bluegrass region of Kentucky.

The more fertile farmlands along the 444-mile Parkway are devoted to the production of milo (a type of sorghum), soybeans, corn, wheat, and cotton, while marginal agricultural lands are used primarily for grazing cattle and horses.

Natural Wonders

— *	**The Mississippi River at Natchez-Under-the-Hill** (p. 71)
12.1	**Turpin Creek** (p. 78)
12.4	**Loess Bluff** (p. 78)
17.5	**Coles Creek** (p. 79)
18.4	**Bullen Creek** (p. 80)
22.0	**Mud Island Creek** (p. 80)
23.0	**North Fork Coles Creek** (p. 80)
52.4	**Owens Creek Falls** (p. 84)
105.6	**Ross R. Barnett Reservoir Overlook** (p. 88)
122.0	**Cypress Swamp** (p. 90)
122.6	**River Bend** (p. 90)
128.4	**Upper Choctaw Boundary** (p. 91)
130.9	**Yockanookany** (p. 91)
145.1	**Myrick Creek** (p. 91)
154.3	**Holly Hill** (p. 91)
164.3	**Hurricane Creek** (p. 93)
175.6	**Cole Creek** (p. 93)
176.3	**Bethel Mission** (p. 93)
193.1	**Jeff Busby Park** (p. 95)
201.3	**Ballard Creek** (p. 96)
203.5	**Pigeon Roost** (p. 96)
243.1	**Davis Lake** (p. 98)
251.9	**Black Belt Overlook** (p. 99)
266.0	**Parkway Visitor Center and Headquarters** (p. 103)
275.2	**Dogwood Valley** (p. 106)
283.3	**Donivan Slough** (p. 106)
286.3	**Browns Bottom** (p. 106)
304.5	**Tishomingo State Park** (p. 108)
313.0	**Bear Creek** (p. 109)
317.0	**Freedom Hills Overlook** (p. 109)
320.3	**Buzzard Roost Spring** (p. 110)
328.7	**Water Route Overlook** (p. 115)
330.2	**Rock Spring** (p. 116)
343.5	**Cypress Creek** (p. 117)
346.2	**Holly** (p. 117)
363.0	**Sweetwater Branch** (p. 117)
364.5	**Glenrock Branch** (p. 118)
377.8	**Jacks Branch** (p. 119)
386.6	**English Camp Branch** (p. 121)
391.9	**Fall Hollow** (p. 123)
392.5	**Swan View Overlook** (p. 123)
394.0	**Devil's Backbone State Natural Area** (p. 123)
404.7	**Jackson Falls** (p. 125)

* Indicates that the point of interest is located before the official start of the Natchez Trace Parkway.

THE LIVING TRACE

All life used this Trace, and he liked to see the animals move along it in direct, oblivious journey, for they had begun it and made it, the buffalo and deer and the small running creatures before man ever knew where he wanted to go.

—Eudora Welty, "A Still Moment"

The Living Trace category is a way to consider the lives of people who have lived and worked alongside the Trace over many years. Only now and again can we catch glimpses of the experiences, customs, and everyday routines of these people.

Some, such as those who built the **Windsor Ruins,** were rich, but most others led commonplace, sometimes hardscrabble, lives. The town of **Rocky Springs,** for example, thrived for decades, but now only a few relics remain: two safes that were probably too heavy to move and a church that still gathers the faithful. **Witch Dance** still keeps alive a different kind of belief: where witches dance, the grass turns brown. **French Camp** began as a trading post but early on became a school.

Tennessee's **Gordon House** and the more contemporary **Tobacco Farm** are the structures of families whose primary sustenance came from the land itself. Rather than just passing through, these people attached themselves to the region because of what it had to offer: a chance to succeed in spite of inevitable change.

Trace Tip

The major bridges in the list below point to other kinds of changes—improvements that would make any ancient Trace foot- or horse-traveler howl with envy for the ease that the bridges' engineered spans provide.

The Living Trace

NATIONAL PARK SERVICE (NPS) INFORMATION

For more than two decades it was the most significant highway of the Old Southwest and one of the most important in the nation. It was an avenue of exploration, international rivalry, warfare, trade, settlement, and development. This old road . . . recalls an early and heroic chapter in our national epic.

> —Dawson Phelps, *An Administrative History of the Natchez Trace Parkway*

For help in sorting out the many stories of the Old Trace, the **Parkway Visitor Center** (2680 Natchez Trace Parkway, Tupelo; 800–305–7417 or 662–680–4027, nps.gov/natr), which is also the Parkway's administrative headquarters, is a must. Located near the midpoint of the Parkway, at milepost 102.4, this stop has the most complete interpretive overview of the Trace's history and touring options. It also has Trace-related books, music, and gifts for sale, as well as restrooms and a knowledgeable staff. The Parkway Visitor Center is open daily, 9 a.m.–4:30 p.m. year-round, except Thanksgiving, December 25, and January 1.

Mount Locust Historic Inn and Plantation, at milepost 15.5 in Natchez, is open Thursday–Sunday, 9 a.m.–4:30 p.m., except as noted above.

The **Parkway Information Cabin** is located in the town of Ridgeland, Mississippi, at milepost 102.4 just north of Jackson. It's open Friday and Saturday, 9 a.m.–4 p.m., except as noted above.

The **Meriwether Lewis Visitor Information Center,** in Hohenwald, Tennessee, at milepost 385.9, is open seasonally, generally spring–fall; call or check the website above for the latest information.

While other contact and ranger stations are marked on maps, you shouldn't expect to find interpretive or other services there.

National Park Service (NPS) Information

Morning fog shrouds the Tennessee River just off the Natchez Trace Parkway. Photo: marekuliasz/Shutterstock

CHAPTER 2
The Nuts and Bolts of Traveling the Trace

> Surrounded on each side with a deep wall of woods, I enjoyed the serenity of the evening in silent meditation: everything I saw and heard taught me a lesson which required not the powers of oratory to embellish it.
>
> —*Francis Bailey, Trace traveler in 1797*

HOW TO USE THE MILEPOSTS

The Trace is a wonderful way to loosen yourself from everyday constraints as its rhythms lull you into imagining what life was like here over thousands of years. Every so often, though, it helps to know where you are on the 444-mile stretch.

Trace Tip

For tips on bicycling the Parkway, see nps.gov/natr/planyourvisit/bicyclinghome.htm.

Each mile of the Trace is marked on the right–hand side heading north, or on the left–hand side heading south, by unobtrusive brown posts with a yellow engraved number). The miles run south–north, just as they would've been experienced by the thousands of Kaintucks, the boatmen from the mid-South and above, who walked or rode a horse north on the Trace toward home. The mileposts can help you calculate how far you have to go until the next crossroad or the next place to stop and see something special along the Trace.

PARKWAY RULES

- ▲ Nonrecreational hauling and commercial trucking are not allowed.
- ▲ Tent and trailer camping are permitted only at designated campgrounds.
- ▲ All natural, historical, and archaeological objects are protected by federal law.
- ▲ Build fires only in fire rings and grills.
- ▲ The Natchez Trace Parkway is a designated bike route; watch for cyclists and yield when necessary.
- ▲ All-terrain vehicles are prohibited on the Parkway.
- ▲ Report all accidents, fires, and emergencies to the nearest park ranger.

FIREARMS

Anyone who is legally entitled to own firearms may possess them on the Parkway, provided they also comply with all applicable laws for carrying and transporting them.

In context of the Natchez Trace and the National Park Service (NPS), federal law prohibits carrying firearms (1) inside of any building owned or leased by the US government and (2) in any national cemetery. Any firearm that is prohibited by state or federal law is also prohibited on the Parkway.

State gun laws applicable on the Parkway are as follows:

MISSISSIPPI (MILEPOSTS 0.0–310.0) Any firearm that is legal to possess under state or federal law may be carried in your vehicle without a permit, whether or not it is loaded or concealed. Open and concealed carry outside of your vehicle do not require a permit as long as the firearm is in a holster, *except* (1) in places where firearms are prohibited by federal law, (2) in bars and the bar areas of restaurants, (3) in places of worship, and (3) in any establishment that prohibits firearms and clearly posts notice thereof.

ALABAMA (MILEPOSTS 310.0–344.0) Any firearm that is legal to possess under state or federal law may be carried in your vehicle without a permit as long as it is unloaded and stored inside a locked compartment; carrying a loaded gun in your car requires a permit. Open carry outside of your vehicle does not require a permit as long as the firearm is in a holster; concealed carry requires a permit. Both open and concealed carry are prohibited in places where firearms are prohibited by federal law.

TENNESSEE (MILEPOSTS 344.0–444.0) Any firearm, loaded or not, that is legal to possess under state or federal law may be carried in your personal vehicle without a permit as long as it is not on your person. Carrying a handgun, concealed or not, outside of your vehicle requires a permit and is prohibited altogether (1) in places where firearms are prohibited by federal law, (2) in places that serve alcohol *unless* the gun owner abstains from drinking, and (3) in any establishment that prohibits firearms and clearly posts notice thereof.

EMERGENCIES

If an emergency arises while you're on the Parkway, call 911 or 800-300-PARK (7275). Provide the nearest milepost if you know it.

A LITTER-FREE TRACE

Please make life easier for the Parkway's outstanding maintenance staff. Garbage cans are located at some stops, but overall the Parkway encourages visitors to pack it in and pack it out. Recycling facilities are available at the **Parkway Visitor Center** in Tupelo and at the **Parkway Information Cabin** in Ridgeland.

SPEEDING ALONG ON THE PARKWAY

A speed limit of 50 mph is strictly enforced on the Parkway. Rangers have no qualms about writing tickets—and just because you don't see any patrol cars on the road doesn't mean that no rangers are on duty.

Trace Tip

Note that speeding here is a federal violation. Fines can be as expensive as $600 as of 2019.

The rewards of obeying the speed limits are twofold. First, the point of traveling the Trace is to enjoy the scenery, and slowing down from the usual 70-plus miles per hour on the interstate makes a measurable difference in your ability to take in all that the countryside has to offer. Second, a slower pace helps you notice potential traffic hazards, including bikers, motorcyclists, and wildlife, and react in a timely manner.

TIMING YOUR TRIP

In 2018 the Parkway logged more than 6 million recreational visits to its roughly 52,000 total acres—making it one of the top 10 most-visited parks in the National Park System. Most visitors travel in the fall and spring, but the Trace never feels crowded. It's possible, in fact, to see just 10 cars in 30 miles on a gorgeous spring day.

WEATHER AND CLIMATE

Spring and fall attract visitors when the weather is more temperate. Winter is usually cold and damp, with occasional warm periods. Summer tends to be very hot and humid, even more so the closer you get to Natchez.

For Trace travelers in the early 19th century, weather was the greatest obstacle to comfortable travel. Dr. Rush Nutt, a planter and physician, noted in his diary: "Rains annually commence in January and February which causes all the creeks to overflow the lowlands, and continue high until March or April, during which time the traveler meets with considerable difficulty in passing them."

In wet weather, the swamps at various points along the Trace were almost impassable and constituted one of the greatest hazards of Old Trace travel. In especially wet periods, some portions of the Parkway can still become impassable due to water.

Long-gone Trace traveler Adam Hodgson wrote of plunging in some swamps "up to the saddle-skirts in mire at every step. The bottom is stiff clay, and horses sometimes stick so fast that they cannot be extricated, but are left to die."

Trace Tip

When planning your trip, find weather shelters along the Parkway by visiting nps.gov/natr /planyourvisit/weather.htm.

Tornadoes could make the Trace an indiscernible, impervious thicket, and Learner Blackman was one of those few travelers who experienced a snowstorm on the Trace long ago: "I was as near frozen as I ever was in my life," he wrote. "The snow became near a foot deep, and the Trace having been softened by a recent rain, we could not walk to warm ourselves and had to sit on our horses and bear the cold as best we could."

Count your present-day creature-comfort blessings, but do roll down the windows and breathe in the benefits of the Parkway as befits the season.

WHAT TO WEAR

Of course, vacation enjoyment dictates comfortable clothing, and the key here is footwear. Closed-toe shoes are highly recommended if you want to do any off-pavement walking. Although the many short nature trails are generally well kept, some have long grasses, so sturdy shoes are best, particularly for sections of the Old Trace.

HOW SAFE IS THE TRACE?

Good sense is always a critical ingredient for safe travel. You needn't fear bandits and murderers the way the Old Trace travelers did, but on the other hand it's a bad idea to leave your car unlocked. Still, you shouldn't let the remote possibility of danger deprive you of doing what you want to do: the Parkway has a low crime rate, thanks in large part to the constant patrolling of NPS rangers and local law enforcement.

NATURAL DANGERS

Much more likely than an encounter with a mugger is a run-in with **poison ivy** (*Toxicodendron radicans*), which is found all over the Trace. It can appear as a

Poison ivy Photo: Tom Watson

tree-climbing hairy vine, a ground cover trailing vine, or more rarely as a low shrub. The rhyming rubric "Leaves of three, let it be" is a good guide. Poison ivy can reach out and touch you in every season—it's particularly troublesome when leafless in the late winter and early spring (Google "poison ivy in all four seasons" for additional identification tips).

The best way to prevent a rash is to prevent contact by wearing closed-toe shoes, long pants, and long sleeves. Don't let dogs rummage through poison ivy either: if urushiol (the oil in the plant that causes the rash) has gotten on your pet's fur, chances are good that it will get on you too.

If you know you've been exposed, you need to act quickly. Clean the affected area with rubbing alcohol if you can. Next, rinse with cold water, but don't scrub. Then take a cold shower with regular soap and water—taking a tub bath in warm water will just spread the urushiol around. Cleansers specifically formulated to break down urushiol (such as Tecnu) are available at many drugstores. If you end up with a rash, calamine lotion or cortisone cream can soothe the itch. Finally, make sure to wash your clothes and anything else that may have gotten urushiol on it, pets included.

Chiggers are the larvae of *Trombiculae,* known in their adult stages as harvest mites. Reddish-orange but almost impossible to see with the naked eye, chiggers quickly latch on to your legs or feet; then they search for a place to settle and snack, such as your ankles or behind your knees. Brush as many chiggers off your body and clothes as you can; then take a shower at the first opportunity to wash away any that may still be hanging around. Be sure to launder clothes, socks, and other items that may still be harboring

Chigger Photo: Alan R. Walker/CC BY-SA 4.0
(creativecommons.org/licenses/by-sa/4.0)

chiggers. Over-the-counter antihistamines and anti-itch creams can provide relief from the bites of any you missed.

The Trace area has two species of **ticks.** If you should find a lone star tick (*Amblyomma americanum*) or wood tick (*Dermacentor andersoni*) on your body, remove it by grasping it just behind the point of attachment with tweezers or, holding tissue or cloth, use your fingers. Pull straight out using steady pressure. Wash the bite area and apply antiseptic. Tick-borne diseases such as Rocky Mountain spotted fever and erlichosis are a possibility, so watch for fatigue and other health symptoms.

Venomous snakes are another potential danger of which you should be aware along the Trace. Timber rattlesnakes (*Crotalus horridus*), Eastern diamondbacks (*Crotalus adamanteus*), pygmy rattlesnakes (*Sistrurus miliarius*), copperheads (*Agkistrodon contortrix mokasen*), and cottonmouths (*Agkistrodon piscivorus piscivorus*) are all found along the Trace. This is a daunting species list, but you're not likely to encounter any of them, and they bite only if surprised, cornered, or threatened.

Watch carefully where you put your feet along the Parkway's trails. Camouflage is a snake's great ally, and the leafy forest floor is a logical place to stumble upon them. When you step over logs, be especially mindful that a snake isn't snoozing on the far side. Making noise in the woods as you go your way is a good idea, as it spurs the wild ones to give you a wide berth.

White-tailed deer (*Odocoileus virginianus*) are numerous along the Parkway and frequently cross the roadway at inopportune times. Always be on the lookout for them,

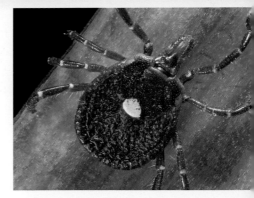

Lone star tick Photo: James Gathany/Centers for Disease Control (public domain)

Wood tick Photo: James Gathany/Centers for Disease Control (public domain)

Timber rattlesnake
Photo: Paul Staniszewski/Shutterstock

especially at dusk. If you see one cross the road, watch and wait for more to follow, as deer are herd animals. Late fall is an especially precarious time, as mating season provokes more movement. Even when you're driving at or under the 50-mph speed limit, a collision with a deer can be very dangerous for all involved.

For more in-depth information on critters, consult *Dangerous Wildlife of the Southeast: A Guide to Safe Encounters at Home and in the Wild,* by F. Lynne Bachleda, one of the authors of this book.

White-tailed deer Photo: BT Images/Shutterstock

CHILDREN'S ACTIVITIES

Pioneer Days provide an opportunity for kids to learn leatherworking, basket making, and other pioneer crafts firsthand from living-history demonstrators. Pioneer Days typically take place at the Parkway Visitor Center, near Tupelo, Mississippi (milepost 266.0), about 10 Saturdays each year. Check out the "Calendar" section at nps.gov/natr, or call 800-305-7417.

Kids ages 6 and up can become **Natchez Trace Parkway Junior Rangers** by completing the activities in a special booklet. By doing word searches, walking on a section of the Old Trace, or asking park rangers about their jobs, kids can learn more about the Parkway and move closer to earning their Junior Ranger badges.

Junior Ranger booklets are available at the following locations:

- ▲ **Mount Locust Historic Inn and Plantation,** milepost 15.5
- ▲ **Parkway Information Cabin,** milepost 102.4
- ▲ **Parkway Visitor Center and Headquarters,** milepost 266.0
- ▲ **Meriwether Lewis Information Center,** milepost 385.9

You can download a copy of the booklet (nps.gov/natr/forkids/beajuniorranger .htm) to start your activities as soon as you get on the Parkway. Completed booklets can be returned to any of the above locations.

GAS, FOOD, AND LODGING

One of the great surprises of being on the Parkway is how far removed civilization can seem, even when it's mere miles away. Numerous crossroads connect you with nearby places to get gas, buy food, and find a room for the night.

Gasoline

There are no gas stations directly on the Parkway, so plan accordingly. The website **Natchez Trace Travel** has detailed information on gas stations nearby: natcheztracetravel.com/gas-stations.

Food

The towns adjacent to the Parkway, especially Tupelo and Jackson, have myriad dining options, from diners and chains to upscale restaurants; check the tourism and visitor-bureau listings in the Appendixes (page 134) for more information. There are, however, also a few special spots where good food and great atmosphere will make your trip more memorable.

Trace Tip

In general you'll need to leave the Parkway to find vittles. A great option is to take a cooler and stop for a picnic along the way.

In **Natchez** you can eat at the **King's Tavern,** built prior to 1789 and purported to be the oldest building in the Natchez Territory. In the early Trace heyday this was the end of the journey for post riders. The combination tavern and post office was a local hangout for Natchez residents and weary travelers until 1820. For protection against outlaws, this was a good place for folks to meet and form groups to walk the Trace together. Of course, the outlaws frequented King's Tavern too.

Used next by the Postlethwaite family as a residence for nearly 150 years, King's Tavern was then purchased by the Pilgrimage Garden Club in 1970 and restored. Today King's Tavern still caters to Parkway adventurers and natives by offering cocktails, seafood, and wood-fired flatbreads and potpies. The building is steeped in history, mystery, and good stories. A jeweled Spanish dagger came to light when a chimney collapsed in early 1900; three skeletons were unearthed from the ground floor in 1930; and reports of ghosts are numerous.

King's Tavern *619 Jefferson St. (at the intersection with Rankin); 601-446-5003, kingstavernnatchez.com. Open Thursday and Friday, 5–10 p.m.; Saturday and Sunday, noon–10 p.m. Entrées start at $15.*

Also in Natchez, have lunch at the **Carriage House Restaurant** on the grounds of **Stanton Hall.** This not-to-be-missed antebellum mansion is now the headquarters for the Pilgrimage Garden Club. (For more information on Stanton Hall and its spring and fall pilgrimages, see "The Millionaires of Natchez," page 68.) Nationally famous, the venue serves a full menu of tasty Southern cooking, including fried chicken, baked ham with raisin sauce, gumbo, homemade salads, and desserts. The biscuits will slay you, and you can enjoy mint juleps in the King's Lounge.

Carriage House Restaurant *401 High St.; 601-445-5151 (no website at press time). Lunch is served Wednesday–Sunday, 11 a.m.–2 p.m.; a full Sunday brunch runs $17.50 for adults.*

Along the Parkway at **French Camp** (milepost 180.7), the **Council House Café,** a ministry of French Camp Academy, is a great place to stop for sandwiches, soups, and a justifiably famous broccoli salad. Sandwiches are made with home-made bread, and you can order fresh Mississippi mud cake or bread pudding for dessert. Enjoy your meal inside a historic log cabin, or sit on the deck.

Council House Café *Milepost 180.7, French Camp; 662-547-9860, frenchcamp historicvillage.com/council-house-cafe. Open Monday–Saturday, 10:30 a.m.–7 p.m.; menu items run $4–$10.*

Tupelo has many places to eat. Stop in at the **Parkway Visitor Center** daily between 9 a.m. and 4:30 p.m. to get recommendations and directions.

David Crockett State Park, just west of Lawrenceburg, Tennessee, has a restaurant that overlooks scenic, 40-acre Lake Lindsey. In addition to a Southern-style buffet, a table-service menu features casual-dining favorites: burgers, sandwiches, salads, pasta, steak, and chicken; there's also a full bar. Check the park's Facebook page (facebook.com/davidcrockettstatepark) for specials.

Crockett's Mill Restaurant *David Crockett State Park, 1400 W. Gaines St.; 831-762-9541, tnstateparks.com/parks/restaurant/david-crockett. Breakfast, Saturday–Sunday, 7:30 a.m.–10 a.m.; lunch, Wednesday–Sunday, 11 a.m.–3 p.m.; dinner, Friday–Saturday, 4 p.m.–8 p.m.; closed Mondays and Tuesdays; entrées run $6–$24.*

In addition to serving delicious Southern food, the Loveless Cafe boasts a diverse array of shops.

At the northern terminus of the Parkway, in **Nashville,** you can partake of what's been a tradition since 1951 at the **Loveless Cafe;** you can see it from the Parkway as you exit on TN 100 going east toward Nashville. The Loveless starts serving their famous breakfasts at 7 a.m. and continues until closing time at 9 p.m. Biscuits, renowned country ham, stone-ground grits, and strong drinks are just a few of the offerings. Supper starts at 11 a.m. with a choice of down-home favorites like fried chicken, catfish, and chicken livers or gizzards. There are salads, soups, sandwich plates, and kid's plates. Sides are too numerous to list. Pies, cobblers, made-from-scratch banana pudding, cupcakes, and vanilla ice cream will finish you off—if the drinks haven't already accomplished that.

Don't be fooled by MOTEL in the name on the old sign. The old motel's rooms have been converted to other businesses, including Hams and Jams country market, Outfitters gift store, the Shipping Shoppe, and Shimai Pottery and Gifts. The Loveless "compound" now also includes an event space known as The Barn.

Loveless Cafe *8400 TN 100; 615-646-9700; lovelesscafe.com. Open daily, 7 a.m.–9 p.m.; entrées run $12–$20.*

Lodging

If it's indoor accommodations you want, consult the Appendixes (page 134) for a listing of nearby motels and hotels, as well as local tourism and visitor-bureau websites that can provide further information. One resource that we recommend highly is **Natchez Trace Travel** (natcheztracetravel.com), a veritable gold mine of information of all kinds about the Trace: food, gas, points of interest, local events, and more. They also offer a bed-and-breakfast directory and reservation service (800-377-2770 or 615-522-4865, natcheztracetravel.com/bedandbreakfasts).

If, however, you prefer to be closer to nature, read on.

CAMPING ALONG THE NATCHEZ TRACE

Following are profiles of the three National Park Service (NPS) campgrounds directly adjacent to the Natchez Trace Parkway from south to north—**Rocky Springs, Jeff Busby,** and **Meriwether Lewis**—along with five state-park campgrounds within 15 miles of the Parkway. Check the Appendixes (page 134) for additional listings, including both public and private options.

The three NPS campgrounds are free. Each campsite has a table, a grill, and a level place to pitch a tent. Restrooms and drinking water are provided; hot water, showers, utility hookups, and dump sites are not. Stays are limited to 14 days. The campgrounds are open year-round, with spring and fall being peak seasons. Organized groups should contact the NPS at 800-305-7417.

Rules and policies are as follows:

- ▲ Campsites are first come, first served.
- ▲ Park only at your campsite.
- ▲ Quiet hours are 10 p.m.–6 a.m.
- ▲ Do not disturb the ground.
- ▲ Please keep your site clean.
- ▲ Build fires only in fireplaces, burn only dead or downed wood, and observe local fire restrictions.
- ▲ Pets are welcome but must be leashed and under control at all times.
- ▲ Fireworks are prohibited, and each Parkway state's firearms policies are in effect (see page 31).

Rocky Springs Campground (Milepost 54.8)

In the 1790s new settlers were attracted to this area by the rich soil and multiple freshwater springs. They cleared the land, constructed homes, and, in 1837, built an impressive brick church still used for worship. By 1860 Rocky Springs was a prosperous rural community of more than 2,000 people, but between 1860 and 1920 the area was devastated by the Civil War, yellow fever, the boll weevil, and land erosion. Today only the church and cemetery, two rusting safes, and abandoned cisterns mark the site.

Rocky Springs offers camping as well as glimpses of history.

The Rocky Springs facility includes the 22-site campground, picnic tables, horseback riding, self-guided trails through the town site and to the spring, and a hiking trail on the Old Trace. Camping and picnicking supplies are available at Port Gibson or Utica, about 15–20 miles away.

Location *On the west side of the Parkway, about 20 miles northeast of Port Gibson, Mississippi.*
GPS: N32° 05.294' W90° 47.931'

Jeff Busby Campground (Milepost 193.1)

This campground is named for Thomas Jefferson Busby, the US Congressman from Mississippi who introduced a bill that resulted in the 1934 act authorizing a survey of the Old Natchez Trace. On May 18, 1938, the Natchez Trace Parkway was authorized as a unit of the National Park System. From here you can walk to Little Mountain, one of Mississippi's highest points on the Parkway at 603 feet above sea level. Jeff Busby Park encompasses an 18-site campground, picnic tables, an exhibit shelter and overlook atop Little Mountain, and a hiking trail.

Location *On the east side of the Parkway, about 33 miles northeast of Kosciusko, Mississippi.* **GPS: N33° 25.068' W89° 16.078'**

Meriwether Lewis Campground (Milepost 385.9)

In 1809 at Grinder's Inn, Meriwether Lewis, cocaptain of the Lewis and Clark expedition and one-time governor of the Upper Louisiana Territory, died of gunshot wounds. A monument, designed as a broken shaft, marks his grave. The facilities include a 32-site campground, a pioneer cemetery, picnic tables, ranger station, exhibits, restrooms, and trails. Camping and picnicking supplies and gasoline are available west of the Parkway on TN 20 in Hohenwald.

Location *On the west side of the Parkway, inside Meriwether Lewis Park and National Monument, Hohenwald, Tennessee, about 80 miles southwest of Nashville.* **GPS: N35° 31.344' W87° 27.332'**

STATE-PARK CAMPGROUNDS WITHIN 15 MILES OF THE PARKWAY

Mississippi Department of Wildlife, Fisheries, and Parks *800-GO-PARKS (467-2757), mdwfp.com/parks-destinations*

Mississippi State Parks charge a day-use fee of $4 per private vehicle for up to six people, plus an extra 50¢ per person above that; pedestrians and cyclists are charged 50¢ per person. Charges for specific activities may apply. A state license is required to fish for persons ages 16–64 (buy online at mdwfp.com/license/fishing; prices vary). Camping fees are $15–$28 per night. Pets are prohibited in cabins and cottages but are welcome at campsites as long as they're on a leash (6 feet maximum) and under control at all times.

Natchez (Milepost 8.1)

Natchez State Park Campground *230-B Wickliff Road, Natchez, MS 39120; 601-442-2658, tinyurl.com/natchezsp*

This campground is 10 miles north of Natchez, the oldest settlement on the Mississippi River. Before the Civil War, more than half of the millionaires in the United States lived in Natchez and constructed opulent mansions, many of which are now open for tours.

Number of campsites 8 primitive tent sites, 50 RV/tent sites (pull-throughs and back-ins)

Each site has Picnic table, grill, and fire ring; RV/tent sites have electrical and water hookups; 6 sites also have sewer hookups

Cabins 10 air-conditioned lakeside cabins with bed and bath linens and basic kitchen equipment

Facilities Dump station, restrooms, hot showers

Reservations Online at mississippistateparks.reserveamerica.com (click "Find Camping Spot" and type in "Natchez State Park")

Other Natchez Lake stocked for fishing; picnic area 0.5 mile from lake has 10 tables and grills; pavilion available for rent

Directions From the Parkway exit at milepost 8.1, 10 miles north of Natchez in Stanton, Mississippi, take US 61 East 1.4 miles, and turn right (south) onto State Park Road. In 0.4 mile turn left onto Wickliff Road; in another 0.4 mile turn right (south) at the park entrance, and drive about 1.7 miles farther to reach the campground. **GPS: N31° 35.852' W91° 12.981'**

Tupelo (Milepost 259.7)

Trace State Park Campground *2139 Faulkner Road, Belden, MS 38826; 662-489-2958, tinyurl.com/tracestatepark*

Located about 9 miles northwest of Tupelo, one of Mississippi's fastest-growing cities, Trace State Park offers a variety of outdoor activities, from fishing and water sports to hiking on miles of trails. A special arrangement with Pontotoc Country Club lets park guests enjoy the club's 18-hole golf course without paying greens fees.

Number of campsites 10 primitive tent sites, 17 primitive group sites, 70 RV/tent sites (pull-throughs and back-ins)

Each site has Picnic table, grill, and fire ring; primitive group areas have water and electrical hookups; RV/tent sites also have sewer hookups

Cabins 6 air-conditioned cabins and 3 air-conditioned cottages with bed and bath linens, basic kitchen equipment, outdoor grills, and porches overlooking Trace Lake

Facilities Dump station, restrooms, hot showers in developed camping area; picnic area and bathhouse near primitive camping area

Reservations Online at mississippistateparks.reserveamerica.com (click "Find Camping Spot" and type in "Trace State Park")

Other Trace Lake stocked for fishing and available for water sports; boat rentals and launches; 25 picnic sites throughout park with tables and grills; 35 miles of trails for use by ATVs, motorcycles (helmets required), horses, and mountain bikes

Directions From the Parkway exit at milepost 259.7 in Tupelo, head west on Pontotoc Parkway/US 278/MS 6. In 6.2 miles turn right (north) onto Black

Zion Road. In 0.6 mile make a quick jog right onto Main Street; then take the next left onto northbound Faulkner Road/CR 65. In 2.1 miles, turn right onto CR 61 to reach the park entrance. The camping loops are located on the north shore of Trace Lake along CR 61. **GPS: N34° 15.618' W88° 53.187'**

Tupelo (Milepost 263.6)

Tombigbee State Park Campground *264 Cabin Drive, Tupelo, MS 38804; 662-842-7669, tinyurl.com/tombigbeestatepark*

Located just 6 miles south of Tupelo, Tombigbee State Park offers outdoor recreation opportunities minutes from town. A scenic ridge overlooking Lake Lee provides the ideal spot for tent camping.

Number of campsites 4 primitive tent sites, 3 primitive group sites, 20 RV/tent sites (back-ins only)

Each site has Picnic table, grill, and fire ring; RV/tent sites have electrical and water hookups; 18 sites also have sewer hookups; primitive sites also have swings and wooden hammock stands

Cabins 7 rustic air-conditioned cabins and 1 ADA-accessible cottage with bed and bath linens, basic kitchen equipment, a fireplace, and a screened porch or patio

Facilities Dump station, restrooms, hot showers in developed camping area; picnic tables and bathhouse near primitive camping area

Reservations Online at mississippistateparks.reserveamerica.com (click "Find Camping Spot" and type in "Tombigbee State Park")

Other Lake Lee stocked for fishing and available for water sports; fishing and paddleboat rentals; 37 lakeside picnic sites throughout park with tables and grills; 2 picnic pavilions; 18-hole disc golf course; 3 nature trails

Directions From the Parkway exit at milepost 263.6 in Tupelo, head east on McCullough Boulevard/MS 6, drive 1.7 miles, and bear left at the fork to merge onto US 45 South. In 1.1 miles exit onto US 278/MS 6 West/East Main Street; in another 1.2 miles, turn right to continue on US 278/MS 6 West/Briar Ridge Road. In 2.5 miles turn left (east) onto CR 1050; then, in 0.7 mile, turn left again and continue east on State Park Road. Drive 1.7 miles farther, and then turn right onto Cabin Drive to enter the park. The camping loops are located on the south side of Lake Lee along Cabin Drive. **GPS: N34° 13.985' W88° 37.830'**

Tishomingo (Milepost 303.9)

Tishomingo State Park Campground *105 CR 90, Tishomingo, MS 38873; 662-438-6914, tinyurl.com/tishomingostatepark*

According to Mississippi Wildlife, Fisheries, and Parks, archaeological excavations confirm that American Indians lived in the area that is now the state park as early as 7000 BC. The Natchez Trace Parkway runs directly through the park, which is named after a legendary Chickasaw chief.

Number of campsites 17 primitive tent sites, 62 RV/tent sites (back-ins only)

Each site has Picnic table, grill, and fire ring; RV/tent sites have electrical and water hookups; each RV pad offers direct access to Haynes Lake

Cabins 6 rustic air-conditioned cabins and 1 ADA-accessible cottage overlooking Bear Creek; all have bed and bath linens, basic kitchen equipment, a fireplace, and a screened porch or patio

Facilities Dump station, restrooms, hot showers in developed camping area; picnic tables and bathhouse near primitive camping area

Reservations Online at mississippistateparks.reserveamerica.com (click "Find Camping Spot" and type in "Tishomingo State Park"); primitive sites are first come, first served

Other Haynes Lake stocked for fishing; fishing-boat rentals; swimming pool with shower facilities; float trips down Bear Creek; 50 picnic sites throughout park with tables and grills; 3 picnic pavilions with electricity; 13-mile trail system; 3 (18-hole) disc golf courses and a compass course; rock climbing

Directions From the Parkway exit at milepost 303.9 in Dennis, head north on MS 25 and, in 0.5 mile, turn right (east) onto State Park Road/CR 90. In 1.8 miles, turn left (north) to access the campground road. The campsites are located along the west and north shores of Haynes Lake.

GPS: N34° 36.700' W88° 12.060'

Tennessee State Parks *888-TN-PARKS (867-2757), tnstateparks.com*

Camping fees are $11–$35 per day. Pets welcome at campsites; must be leashed, cleaned up after, and under control at all times.

Lawrenceburg (Milepost 369.9)

David Crockett State Park Campground *1400 W. Gaines St., Lawrenceburg, TN 38464; 931-762-9408, tnstateparks.com/parks/david-crockett*

Dedicated in May 1959 in honor of one of Tennessee's most famous native sons, David Crockett State Park is 0.5 mile west of Lawrenceburg. A pioneer, soldier, politician, and industrialist, David Crockett was born near Limestone in northeast Tennessee in 1786. In 1817 he moved to Lawrence County, where he served as a justice of the peace, militia leader, and state legislator.

According to Tennessee State Parks, Crockett established a powder mill, grist-mill, and distillery along Shoal Creek on land that is now occupied by the park, but all three were washed away in an 1821 flood. Crockett subsequently moved to western Tennessee, where he was elected to Congress. He died March 6, 1836, at The Alamo in San Antonio, helping Texans battle for independence from Mexico.

Number of campsites Campground 1: 10 primitive tent sites, 45 RV/tent sites (pull-throughs and back-ins); Campground 2: 52 RV/tent sites (back-ins only)

Each site has Picnic table, grill, and fire ring; RV/tent sites have electrical and water hookups

Cabins 7 LEED-certified, furnished cabins (1 is pet-friendly), each with 2 bedrooms, 2 baths, a full kitchen, a gas fireplace, and a covered patio

Facilities Dump station, restrooms, bathhouses with hot showers

Reservations Online at reserve.tnstateparks.com/david-crockett

Other Lake Lindsey stocked for fishing (license required); paddleboards, canoes, kayaks and fishing boat rentals; swimming pool with shower facilities and concessions; Crockett's Mill Restaurant, overlooking the lake (see page 38); bicycle trail; hiking trails; museum and amphitheater

Directions From the Parkway exit at milepost 369.9, drive east on US 64/TN 15. In 12.8 miles turn left (east) onto West Gaines Street; then, in 2.1 miles, turn left to enter the park. Campground 1 is 0.7 mile farther along the park road, Campground 2 is 1.1 miles north of Campground 1, and the cabin area is 1 mile north of Campground 2 adjacent to Lake Lindsey.
GPS: N35° 14.566' W87° 21.257'

Covered bridge at David Crockett State Park Photo: dansif/Shutterstock

CHAPTER 3
The Many Ways to Travel the Trace

It was the pull and power of the Mississippi River that made the Trace famous, and now the Parkway has a power of its own. Today's travelers have many ways to experience the Natchez Trace.

The Mississippi River remains what it always was, the Nile of the Western Hemisphere.
—John Gunther, journalist, author, and social commentator

MOTORIZED VEHICLES

The most common way of traveling the Parkway today is by car. Nonrecreational commercial hauling is prohibited, but you will see cars hauling camping trailers, as well as trucks pulling horse trailers. RVs are quite common, too, enjoying the more modest speed of 50 miles per hour. RV drivers and those pulling large camping trailers should take heed—a few pull-offs and sections of the Old Trace will not accommodate turnarounds or safe passage.

In some ways it seems the Parkway was made for motorcycles. The open, incredibly scenic roadway summons riders of all ages in what can be a roaring, romantic way to spend an afternoon.

Add bicycles to the mix, and you've got pretty much a full house for accidents, so take care not to get so lost in the scenery in front of you that you lose track of what's near you on the road.

BICYCLES

Touring bikes are another common sight on the Parkway. The section nearest Nashville is hilly and curving, but much of the Parkway is generally flatter and more of a straightaway. The general atmosphere here, especially with the absence of trucks, is that of a sunny country back road.

Trace Tip

High-visibility clothing is strongly recommended when biking the Trace.

The National Park Service (NPS) offers extensive information for cyclists at nps.gov /natr/planyourvisit/bicyclinghome.htm.

Bicycling has become an increasingly popular activity on the Natchez Trace Parkway. Although bicycling is permitted with the flow of traffic on the Parkway, extreme caution is advised on sections of the Parkway with heavy commuter traffic, such as those in Tupelo and Jackson, Mississippi. To ensure a safe and enjoyable trip, bicyclists are encouraged to avoid being on the road in Tupelo and Jackson from 7 to 9 a.m. and from 4 to 6 p.m.

The suggested alternative route through Ridgeland and metro Jackson is the **Chisha Foka Multi-Use Trail,** a 10-mile paved path that's pleasant for bicyclists as well as walkers, joggers, people with strollers or in wheelchairs, and dogs on leashes. Visitors can access this trail from the Ross R. Barnett Reservoir Overlook (milepost 105.6), the Old Trace and Brashears Stand Site (milepost 104.5), the Choctaw Agency (milepost 100.0), or the Parkway Information Cabin (milepost 102.4).

If you're organizing a group ride, a special-use permit is required; contact the Chief Ranger's Office at 662-680-4014, Monday–Friday, 8 a.m.–4:30 p.m.

Please observe the following safety rules when you're bicycling on the Natchez Trace Parkway:

▲ Obey all traffic regulations.

▲ Keep to the right and ride in a straight line. Always ride single-file.

▲ Never hitch onto other vehicles or race in traffic.

▲ Never carry other riders or items that obstruct vision or prevent proper control of the bicycle.

▲ Be sure your bicycle is in perfect running condition, and your brakes operate efficiently.

▲ Wear a helmet and reflective clothing.

▲ Each bicycle must exhibit a white light on the front and a red light or red reflector on the rear during periods of low visibility or during the period between sundown and sunup.

▲ Always carry drinking water.

▲ Use proper hand signals for turning and stopping.

▲ Plan to be off the Parkway by sundown.

▲ In case of an emergency, call 911 or 800-300-7275.

> ## Trace Tip
>
> The width of the Parkway varies, with a wider right-of-way at areas of historical, scientific, and recreational value. All lands outside of this boundary, with the exception of **Tishomingo State Park** and **Tombigbee National Forest** in northeast Mississippi, are privately owned and require owner permission to use for any purpose.

Drinking water is available at some mileposts, but note that north of Ridgeland, Mississippi (milepost 102.4), the outside drinking fountains are turned off mid-November–mid-March, depending on the weather.

Bicycle Shops near the Parkway

MISSISSIPPI
Natchez

Trippe's Western Auto *180 S. Sergeant Prentiss Drive; 601-445-4186, shoptrippes .com. Open Monday–Saturday, 8 a.m.–6 p.m.*

Jackson Area

The Bike Crossing *115 W. Jackson St., Ridgeland; 601-856-0049, thebikecrossing .tripod.com. Open Monday–Friday, 10 a.m.–7 p.m.; Saturday, 10 a.m.–5 p.m.*

Indian Cycle Fitness & Outdoor *677 S. Pear Orchard Road, Ridgeland; 601-956-8383, indiancyclefitness.com. Open Monday–Saturday, 10 a.m.–6 p.m.*

Ride South *105 Avalon Court, Brandon; 601-992-2490, ridesouth.com. Open Tuesday–Friday, 10 a.m.–6 p.m.; Saturday, 10 a.m.–5 p.m.*

Tupelo

Bicycle Pacelines *2120 W. Jackson St.; 662-844-8660, bicyclepacelines.net. Open Monday–Friday, 11 a.m.–6 p.m.; Saturday, 10 a.m.–4 p.m.*

Core Cycle and Outdoors *1697 N. Coley Road; 662-260-5266, corecycleand outdoor.com. Open Monday–Saturday, 9:30 a.m.–6 p.m.*

Trails and Treads *549 N. Coley Road; 662-690-6620, facebook.com/trailsand treads. Open Monday–Friday, 10 a.m.–6 p.m.; Saturday, 9 a.m.–5 p.m.*

ALABAMA
Florence

The Spinning Spoke Cycle Hub *221 N. Seminary St.; 256-349-5302, spinning spoke.com. Open Monday–Friday, 10 a.m.–6 p.m.; Saturday, 9 a.m.–5 p.m.*

TENNESSEE
Columbia

The Spinning Spoke Cycle Hub Columbia *11 Public Square; 931-548-8313, spinningspoke.com/trek-columbia. Open Monday–Friday, 10 a.m.–6 p.m.; Saturday, 9 a.m.–6 p.m.*

Franklin

Mac's Harpeth Bikes *1110 Hillsboro Road; 615-472-1002, macsharpethbikes.com. Open Monday–Friday, 10 a.m.–6 p.m.; Thursday, 10 a.m.–7 p.m.; Saturday, 10 a.m.–5 p.m.*

Moab Bicycles *109 Del Rio Pike, Ste. 105; 615-807-2035, moabbikes.com. Open Monday–Friday, 10 a.m.–6 p.m.; Saturday, 10 a.m.–4 p.m.*

Nashville

Cumberland Transit *2807 West End Ave.; 615-321-4069, cumberlandtransit.com. Open Monday–Saturday, 10 a.m.–6 p.m.; Sunday 12 p.m.–5 p.m.*

Trace Bikes *8080-B TN 100 (at the northern terminus); 615-642-2485, tracebikes .com. Open Monday–Friday, 10 a.m.–6 p.m.; Saturday, 10 a.m.–5 p.m.; Sunday, noon–4 p.m. Bike rentals available.*

Bicycle Camping

The Parkway has five nonvehicular campgrounds for use by cyclists, hikers, and Scouts; see the Appendixes (page 134) for more information.

HIKING AND HORSEBACK RIDING

Natchez Trace National Scenic Trail

If you want to experience the Trace area the way the folks who made it famous 200 years ago did, spend some time on foot or horseback. It's a romantic notion that you can still walk or ride the entire forested Old Trace—but you can't. Parts of the Old Trace are lost to time and nature, and some parts of it are on privately owned lands, but the paved Parkway does coincide with a small portion of the old path.

The NPS has made strides to accommodate those who'd rather make their way on foot. The Natchez Trace National Scenic Trail (NTNST) was established on March 28, 1983, as a unit of the National Trails System. More than 60 miles of trail are open for use in five areas along the Natchez Trace Parkway. The best resource to stay current on the National Scenic Trail is scenictrace.com/what-to-do/hiking.

Fairly easy, with few elevation changes and no major obstacles, these trails have been built and maintained primarily by members of the Natchez Trace Trail Conference, Vicksburg Trail Dusters, Student Conservation Association, Boy Scouts of America, and other volunteers. We've also listed the sections that are open to horseback riders.

Portions of the trail follow sections of the original historic Natchez Trace. Hiking and horseback riding along the trail will take you through areas of rolling hills, meadows, pine and hardwood forests, steep ravines, and some creek crossings. The trail is marked with white rectangular or oblique triangle blazes. Side, spur, and loop trails are blazed in blue. Some sections of the trail also follow along the

Parkway road shoulder, interstates, and state roads—use extreme caution when traveling or crossing in these sections.

Be aware that the Parkway right–of–way line, blazed in yellow and marked by signs, is quite narrow, and the trail route often passes very close to this line, which is immediately adjacent to private property. Please respect property owners' rights along the trail route. The official NTNST brochure and map, along with maps for the individual trail sections profiled next, are available at nps.gov/natt/planyour visit/maps.htm.

Trail rules and guidelines are as follows:

▲ Heavy rains can produce muddy trail conditions, but remain on the trail and tread as lightly as possible to prevent further erosion.

▲ Overnight camping requires a special-use permit. Contact the Permit Officer at Parkway Headquarters by calling 662-680-4014 or 800-305-7417.

▲ Carry out all litter.

▲ No campfires are permitted.

▲ Stay on designated trails.

▲ Fireworks are prohibited, and each Parkway state's firearms policies are in effect (see page 31).

▲ Pets must be on a leash (maximum 6 feet) and under physical control at all times.

▲ All motorized vehicles and bicycles are prohibited.

▲ Drink water only from designated sources.

NTNST SECTIONS

The **Potkopinu Trail** follows the original Old Trace for its entire 3-mile length, portions of which include 15-foot walls associated with the so-called Sunken Trace. The Potkopinu section extends from milepost 17.0 to the trailhead at Road 553 (milepost 20.0). Horses are prohibited, and there are several stream crossings.

Near Port Gibson, Mississippi, the 10-mile **Rocky Springs Trail** extends from the Utica–Reganton Road trailhead (milepost 59.0) south to the Owens Creek Falls pull-off (milepost 52.4). Eight miles are open to horses, and 2 miles are pedestrian-only.

The **Yockanookany Trail,** just north of Jackson, Mississippi, is 24 miles long and passes through areas of historical significance and natural beauty. The northern trailhead is located at the Yockanookany pull-off (milepost 130.9). The southern trailhead is at the West Florida Boundary site (milepost 107.9). Along the way the trail passes the River Bend scenic area (Pearl River) and beautiful Cypress Swamp (milepost 122.0).

The **Blackland Prairie Trail** runs 6 miles from the parking lot across the Parkway from the Visitor Center (milepost 266.0) south to West Jackson Street in Tupelo, near milepost 260.8. The trail passes through the Parkway pull-off areas of Old Town Creek and the Chickasaw Village Site.

At the northern end of the Parkway, the **Highland Rim Trail** comprises 24 miles of trail within Leiper's Fork, near Franklin, Tennessee, extending from the Garrison Creek parking area (milepost 427.6) south to TN 50 (milepost 407.9).

Horseback Riding on the NTNST

The best source of information for equestrians is nps.gov/natr/planyourvisit /horseback-riding.htm. It includes camping possibilities and maps of most of the trails profiled in this section. The five trails profiled here vary in length by section from 3.5 miles to 25 miles and are one-way, loop, or figure-eight routes.

Horse trailers are permitted on the Parkway to transport horses for recreational riding (versus commercial purposes) and must be properly equipped with red taillights, red stoplights, and mechanical turn signals. Clearance lights are required on trailers more than 6 feet high.

> ### Trace Tip
> Horses are prohibited along the entire length of the Parkway, except on established equestrian trails.

Trailers carrying more than 1 ton must be properly equipped with brakes that can be applied by the driver of the towing vehicle from its cab and can be applied automatically in case the trailer becomes disconnected.

All trailers must be connected to the towing vehicle with a safety chain or equivalent device and may not exceed a total length of 55 feet in conjunction with the towing vehicle.

The loading and unloading of horses and pack animals is permitted only at designated horse trailheads, or staging areas.

Owners of horses transported to or ridden on any park trail must have in their possession either the original or a copy of an official negative test (Coggins test) for equine infectious anemia administered within the previous 12 months.

In addition to the above, the following rules and guidelines apply:

▲ Horse trails go through mostly wooded terrain.

▲ Trails are for day use only. The NPS website above lists nearby camping options.

▲ Horses are prohibited in camping and picnicking areas.

▲ There are no horse-rental facilities along the Parkway.

▲ Use caution when you must cross the Parkway.

▲ Only one rider per horse is permitted on the trails.

NATCHEZ TRACE HORSE TRAILS

NTNST: ROCKY SPRINGS SECTION This steep, challenging 4-mile horse trail crosses creeks and ravines. The out-and-back trail traverses the National Scenic Trail from the Utica–Reganton Road trailhead (milepost 59.0) to Rocky Springs Campground (milepost 54.8), and riders will cross the Parkway once.

NTNST: YOCKANOOKANY SECTION This 23-mile horse trail begins in Ridgeland, Mississippi. Access the one-way trail from the Parkway at MS 43 (milepost 114.9). A gravel parking area with limited space is located on the north access leg of MS 43. Travel north (16 miles) to the terminus at milepost 130.9 or south (approximately 7 miles) to the West Florida Boundary at milepost 107.9.

TOMBIGBEE NATIONAL FOREST: WITCH DANCE HORSE TRAIL This 18-mile multiloop trail lies almost entirely within the national forest adjacent to the Parkway. Access the trail from the Parkway at the Witch Dance trailhead and picnic area (milepost 233.2), 6 miles south of MS 32 and 4 miles north of MS 8. A paved parking and staging area is opposite the restrooms.

Footbridge on the
Witch Dance Horse Trail in
Tombigbee National Forest
Photo: Fredlyfish4/Shutterstock

NTNST: BLACKLAND PRAIRIE SEGMENT This loop trail, 3.5 miles in length, is northwest of Tupelo, Mississippi, within the boundaries of the Parkway. Access it from the Parkway at MS 6 (milepost 260.0). Travel west on MS 6 to Air Park Road; then turn north (right) and east (right) onto Jackson Street. A paved parking and staging area is on the left.

NTNST: HIGHLAND RIM SEGMENT This horse trail, about 25 miles long, is 1 mile south of TN 46 near the town of Leiper's Fork, within the boundaries of the Parkway. The trail parallels the Parkway from the Garrison Creek parking and staging area (milepost 427.6) to the TN 50 parking and staging area (milepost 408.0).

Milepost Trails

The self-guided trails you'll find along the milepost stops are pleasant, often charming leg stretches, but no self-respecting hiker or even walker would suggest they're anything more than that. Most take a maximum of 15–30 minutes to experience at full stroll.

Listed below are additional hiking opportunities that are linked to milepost stops (in parentheses):

- ▲ **Coles Creek (17.5)** Follow the path of the Old Trace for 3.5 miles through flat lowland forest.
- ▲ **Rocky Springs (54.8)** At times following the Old Trace, this trail is 10 miles long. The terrain has some roll to it, but nothing strenuous.
- ▲ **Jeff Busby (193.1)** A 1-mile trek to the overlook at Little Mountain has a few uphill stretches. Alternatively, you could take a more leisurely walk along the road to the same vista.
- ▲ **Witch Dance (233.2)** More than 10 miles of trails are shared with horses, which have a tendency to leave rough surfaces for human feet, especially after a good rain.
- ▲ **Parkway Visitor Center, Tupelo (266.0)** A 4.5-mile trail connects to the Old Town Overlook (263.9) and then goes on to the Chickasaw Village Site (261.8). The terrain is flat past fields and into forests.
- ▲ **Tishomingo State Park (304.5)** Here, 13 miles of trails explore the southern foothills of the Appalachian Mountains. This area has massive rocks that are unusual for the Trace area, as well as mature hardwoods. Hike along Bear Creek or explore ridgetops with moderate difficulty.
- ▲ **Meriwether Lewis Park and National Monument (385.9)** This NPS historic site, park, and campground has more than 5 miles of trails, some of which run concurrently with the Old Trace. Ridges and hollows along Little Swan Creek make for moderately difficult hiking.
- ▲ **Devil's Backbone State Natural Area (394.0)** More than 3 miles of trails wind through a hardwood forest. Traversing ridges and valleys, these moderately difficult hikes visit creeks and waterfalls.
- ▲ **Garrison Creek (427.6)** Its 25 miles of moderately difficult trails (shared with horses) climb ridges, overlook fields, and ford creeks.

Nearby State-Park Hiking Trails

In addition to the sites above, the following state parks along the Trace, listed north–south, offer hiking opportunities.

▲ **Natchez State Park (Mississippi)** Choose from several out-and-back hikes along old logging roads, ranging 0.25–2.8 miles one-way. *230-B Wickliff Road, Natchez; 601-442-2658, tinyurl.com/natchezsp.*

▲ **Trace State Park (Mississippi)** Its 25 miles of trails are shared with ATVs, dirt bikes, mountain bikes, and horses. *2139 Faulkner Road, Belden; 662-489-2958, tinyurl.com/tracestatepark.*

▲ **Tombigbee State Park (Mississippi)** Three nature trails vary in length from 0.5 to 1.2 miles. *264 Cabin Drive, Tupelo; 662-842-7669, tinyurl.com /tombigbeestatepark.*

▲ **David Crockett State Park (Tennessee)** The 5 miles of trails include a paved bike trail and a moderately difficult trek through a maple-and-oak forest. *1400 W. Gaines St., Lawrenceburg; 931-762-9408, tnstateparks.com/parks/david-crockett.*

Trace Tip

For detailed information about hikes in the Tennessee section of the Trace, consult Johnny Molloy's *60 Hikes Within 60 Miles: Nashville* (Menasha Ridge Press).

WATER

Many of the milepost stops have a water element. Most, however, are for visual delight rather than immersion. The NPS advises against swimming, but there are some nice creeks where you can chill your dogs on a hot summer day by wading or dangling your toes from a sunny rock perch. **Metal Ford** (milepost 382.8), for example, is a fairly broad, flat-bottomed stretch of the Buffalo River.

As for canoeing, there are several possibilities. If you've got your own boat, **River Bend** (milepost 122.6) is a flatwater paddle in a swampy area. It's at the northern end of Ross R. Barnett Reservoir, the largest lake along the Parkway.

For more information about paddling in Mississippi, check with **Buffalo Peak Outfitters** in Jackson (601-366-2557 or 800-232-2503, buffalopeak.net).

Near the Mississippi–Alabama state line, **Tishomingo State Park** (milepost 304.5) offers the **Bear Creek Canoe Float Trip** ($40 per person) in warmer months. This 6.25-mile trip down rocky-bottomed Bear Creek operates daily, mid–April–mid–October. Trips leave from the swinging bridge at 10 a.m. Participants must register at the park office 30 minutes before departure and return to the swinging bridge about 2.5–3 hours later. Call the park office at 662-438-6914 for reservations.

For a host of water-recreation options, including fishing, sailing, and water skiing, check out **Ross R. Barnett Reservoir,** just north of Jackson, Mississippi. For

Metal Ford (milepost 382.9, page 120) makes a great stop in spring or at any time of year.

more information, check out milepost 105.6 in Chapter 5 (see page 88). The Tennessee River at **Colbert Ferry,** milepost 327.3, also has boat launches.

Finally, of course, we'd be remiss if we didn't recommend just watching the mighty Mississippi roll by at **Natchez** or **Vicksburg.**

ACCESSIBLE AREAS FOR PEOPLE WITH DISABILITIES

The Parkway is a mixed bag when it comes to accessibility. On the upside, much of the Trace can be experienced and enjoyed by car; on the downside, only a few of the self-guided milepost trails (see page 55) are paved and thus reliably easy for wheelchair users to navigate. Many of these trails, however, are short enough that an ambulatory companion can scout the terrain first to see if it's doable.

Most restrooms are accessible (marked in blue on the official map), as are all parking areas at the visitor center and contact stations.

Trace Tip

For detailed information about accessible facilities by milepost, visit nps.gov/natr/planyourvisit /accessibility.htm.

CHAPTER 4
A Chronology of the Natchez Trace

The Natchez Trace is a route replete with history.

OVERVIEW

In the following chapter we list some of the historical highlights of this uniquely American byway.

Discovery of the Mississippi (1853) by William Henry Powell, commissioned for the Rotunda of the US Capitol, depicts a key event in Hernando de Soto's exploration of the American South in the 16th century. Photo: Architect of the Capitol (public domain)

1540–1541   Hernando de Soto spends part of the winter in Chickasaw villages in Mississippi.

1682   René-Robert Cavelier, Sieur de La Salle, visits the Natchez tribe.

1699   South Carolina settlers begins trading with the Chickasaw.

1700   Pierre Le Moyne d'Iberville, the French governor of Louisiana, meets the Natchez tribe.

1710   An unknown French trader sets up business at French Lick, the future site of Nashville, Tennessee.

1716   Fort Rosalie is built at Natchez, Mississippi by Jean Baptiste Le Moyne, Sieur de Bienville.

1718   The French begin to develop several plantations near Natchez.

1729   The Natchez Indians massacre the French colony at Natchez.

1730–31   With the help of the Choctaw, the French avenge the massacre and send the Natchez into exile.

1736   The French attempt to defeat the Chickasaw, but Pierre D'Artaguette is defeated at Ogoula Tchetota, as is Bienville at Ackia.

1739–1740   The French lead an expedition against the Chickasaw. One hundred French Canadians with Indian allies travel from Montreal to Tupelo.

1748–1752   Choctaw Civil War; South Carolina attempts to bring Choctaw under British control.

1763   France cedes North American possessions east of the Mississippi River, except New Orleans, including the Natchez District, to Great Britain. Spain cedes Florida to Great Britain.

1764   Natchez becomes a part of the British Colony of West Florida.

1765–1779   English-speaking people, veterans of the French and Indian War, and exiled Tories from the 13 original colonies settle the Natchez district.

1770   John McIntosh, British agent to Chickasaw and Choctaw Indians, establishes his agency, Tockshish, or McIntoshville, 10 miles south of Pontotoc.

1775–1783   The American Revolution marks the struggle by which the 13 colonies win independence from Great Britain. The fighting ends when Cornwallis surrenders at Yorktown in October.

1779   Spanish Colonial forces occupy Natchez.

1779–1782   Mount Locust plantation is built on a Spanish land grant near Natchez.

1780   Nashville is established by Richard Henderson, John Donelson, James Robertson, and other North Carolina settlers.

1781   English-speaking settlers in Natchez revolt against Spain.

1782   Americans of Cumberland settlement and Chickasaw Indians create an alliance.

1783   The Treaty of Paris ends the American Revolution and recognizes the United States as a nation; the Mississippi River becomes the western boundary of the United States; East and West Florida are ceded to Spain; Spain and the United States begin a boundary quarrel.

1785   The first cargo of American goods reaches Natchez via the Ohio and Mississippi Rivers. The first of thousands of boatmen begin their journey over the Natchez Trace to Nashville and other areas in the Ohio Valley.
    A French officer named Chachare, in Spanish service, makes the trip from Natchez to Nashville on the Natchez Trace. His is the first written report of a complete journey over the Trace.

The Natchez assault on the French military post at Fort Rosalie is depicted in John J. Egan's painting *Panorama of the Monumental Grandeur of the Mississippi Valley* (circa 1850).
Photo: St. Louis Art Museum, Eliza McMillan Trust (public domain)

1790 Tennessee, with the tentative name Territory Southwest of the Ohio River, is organized as a Territory of the United States.

1792 Stephen Minor's trip on the Natchez Trace results in a detailed diary.

1795 Spain signs Pinchney's Treaty, agreeing on the 31st Parallel as the southern boundary of the United States; first cotton gin comes to Natchez.

1796 Tennessee is admitted to the Union.

1798 Spain withdraws troops and US forces occupy the Natchez District; the Mississippi Territory is organized, with Natchez as its capital.

1800 Congress establishes a post route between Nashville and Natchez.

1801 The Treaty of Chickasaw Bluffs is signed, affirming that the US may open a road, the Natchez Trace, through Chickasaw lands; the capital of the Mississippi Territory moves from Natchez to Ishington, Mississippi.

1801–02 US troops open the Natchez Trace from Davidson–Williamson County line in Tennessee to Grindstone Ford in Mississippi.

1802 The Old Trace in Tennessee between Nashville and Duck River Ridge is abandoned as a post road. George Colbert establishes a ferry across the Tennessee River from Mississippi to Alabama, William Smith establishes Red Bluff Stand in Mississippi, and John Gordon establishes a ferry on the Duck River in Tennessee.

1803 Port Gibson, Mississippi, is founded; the Regiment of Tennessee Militia marches on the Trace to and from Natchez.

1804 The Mississippi territorial boundary is extended north to the Tennessee line; the notorious Trace outlaw, Wiley "Little" Harpe, is executed.

Meriwether Lewis died under mysterious circumstances on the Trace.

Photo: Upper Snake River Valley Historical Society/ CC BY 2.0 (creativecommons.org/licenses/by/2.0)

1805 The Chickasaw cede Tennessee lands between Duck River Ridge and the Buffalo–Duck River watershed to the US; the Old Trace from Duck River Ridge to today's Meriwether Lewis National Monument becomes the boundary between the US and Chickasaw lands. Later the same year, the Choctaw cede their lands south of Old Three-Chopped Way to the US.

1806 The first Congressional appropriation is made for the improvement of the Natchez Trace; Brashears Stand is established by Turner Brashears, who lived among the Choctaw Indians in Mississippi as a trader for nearly 20 years.

1807 Aaron Burr is arrested near Natchez; Silas Dinsmore moves the Choctaw Agency to a site on the Natchez Trace.

1808 The Trace between Duck River Ridge and Buffalo River is abandoned as a post route.

1809 Meriwether Lewis dies and is buried at Grinder's Stand along the Old Trace in Tennessee.

1810 Settlers in the West Florida Territory revolt against Spanish rule.

1812 The first Mississippi River steamboat reaches Natchez from Pittsburgh and arrives downriver at New Orleans on January 10; West Florida is added to the Mississippi Territory; William Doak establishes Doaks Stand in Mississippi.

1812 (APPROXIMATELY) Louis LeFleur establishes LeFleur's Stand (aka French Camp) in Mississippi; John McLish, who is part Chickasaw, establishes McLish Stand in Tennessee.

1813 General John Coffee marches a brigade of cavalry over the Trace from Nashville to Natchez; Andrew Jackson marches with his troops from Natchez to Nashville and is given the nickname "Old Hickory."

1814–15 The Natchez Trace is a vitally important link between Washington and New Orleans when the latter is threatened by British troops and ships.

1815 After the Battle of New Orleans, Jackson's army returns in the spring to Tennessee via the Old Natchez Trace; Steele's Iron Works begins to produce iron at a site on the Buffalo River near the Old Trace in Tennessee.

Andrew Jackson used the Trace as a travel route after his troops were ordered home to Tennessee during the War of 1812. Photo: Library of Congress Prints and Photographs Division (LC-DIG-pga-00295, public domain)

1816 The Treaty of Chickasaw Council House cedes all Chickasaw lands north of the Tennessee River to the United States.

1817 The Alabama Territory is organized; Mississippi becomes the 20th state.

1818 The American Board of Commissioners for Foreign Missions establishes the Choctaw Mission; John Gordon completes his house in Tennessee; the Treaty of Old Town, also known as the Jackson Purchase, cedes Chickasaw lands in Kentucky and Tennessee to the United States.

1819 Alabama becomes the 22nd state.

1820 The Choctaw cede 51.5 million acres of land to the United States in the Treaty of Doaks Stand; the Old Trace between the Buffalo River and Buzzard Roost Stand is abandoned as a post route; Monroe Station of the Chickasaw Mission is established in Pontotoc County, Mississippi.

1820–1830 Steamboat becomes the usual method of travel from Natchez to the northeast.

1821 Bethel, a station of the Choctaw Mission, is established.

1822 The Old Trace between Brashears Stand and Red Bluff Stand is abandoned as a post road.

1830 The Choctaw sign the Treaty of Dancing Rabbit Creek, ceding all lands east of the Mississippi River to the United States and agreeing to move to Oklahoma.

1832 The Chickasaw sign the Treaty of Pontotoc, ceding all lands east of the Mississippi River to the United States and agreeing to move to Oklahoma.

1848 The state of Tennessee erects a monument at the grave of Meriwether Lewis.

1861–65   The Civil War begins when Southern states secede and Confederate commander P. G. T. Beauregard orders his men to fire on Fort Sumter, South Carolina, on April 12, 1861. Four years later, on April 9, 1865, Confederate General Robert E. Lee surrenders to Union General Ulysses S. Grant at the Appomattox Court House in Virginia.

1863   Grant's army marches over the Natchez Trace, from Port Gibson to Raymond.

1864   The Battle of Brices Cross Roads becomes one of Confederate General Nathan Bedford Forrest's most decisive victories; the Union claims a victory in the Battle of Tupelo.

Part of Confederate General John Bell Hood's army marches over the Natchez Trace from the Tennessee–Alabama line to Nashville; after the Battles of Nashville and Franklin, the remainder of Hood's army retreats over the Old Trace to Tupelo, Mississippi.

1909–1933   The route of the Natchez Trace is marked by the Daughters of the American Revolution and other organizations.

1925   The Meriwether Lewis National Monument is established.

1929   The sites of the Battles of Brices Cross Roads and Tupelo are designated as National Battlefields by the US Department of War (now the Department of Defense).

1931   Commemorative monuments are erected at Brices Cross Roads and Tupelo National Battlefields.

1933   Administration of Brices Cross Roads and Tupelo National Battlefields is transferred from the War Department to the National Park Service (NPS).

1934   Congress authorizes a survey of Old Natchez Trace for possible construction of a Natchez Trace Parkway.

This monument was erected in 1931 to commemorate Union and Confederate forces who lost their lives in the Battle of Tupelo in July 1864. Photo: Ken Lund/CC BY 2.0 (creativecommons.org/licenses/by/2.0)

1937 The first construction on the Parkway gets under way in Mississippi.

1938 The Natchez Trace Parkway is created as a unit of the NPS by an act of Congress.

1996 The TN 96 double-arch bridge near Franklin is completed and dedicated, opening the last incomplete section of the Parkway at the northern terminus, near Nashville.

2005 The final segment of the Parkway around Jackson, Mississippi, opens, thereby completing one seamless experience from mileposts 8.1 to 444 and marking 61 years of planning and construction since its modern genesis in 1934. Further plans call for an extension into Natchez and for the construction of a visitor center at the northern terminus near Nashville.

2009 The Parkway Information Cabin (milepost 102.4) reopens at the former Mississippi Craftsmen's Guild.

This double-arch bridge spans Birdsong Hollow, near the end of the Parkway in Tennessee at milepost 438.0 (see page 131). Photo: F. Lynne Bachleda

CHAPTER 5
Sightseeing by Milepost

From Natchez to Nashville, there's plenty to capture your interest along the Trace.

MISSISSIPPI (Mileposts 0.0–308.8)

Natchez

As you might expect, the city of Natchez has several important sites that relate to the Natchez Trace story. Brawling boatmen, antebellum finery, the tragic trade in humans, ancient burial rituals, and the might of the Mississippi River can lure you to stay here at least a day or two. The **City of Natchez** website (natchez.ms.us) is a good place to start. Another good way to get oriented is to contact or stop by the **Natchez Visitor Center** (640 Canal St.; 800-647-6724, visitnatchez.org).

Trace Tip

In this chapter we've included GPS coordinates for a few points of interest that are off the Parkway and could be hard to find, along with the rare Parkway stop that isn't signed. The website **Natchez Trace Travel** (natcheztracetravel.com) lists GPS coordinates for nearly every official stop on the Parkway.

THE MILLIONAIRES OF NATCHEZ

Before the Civil War there were 35 millionaires in the entire United States, and Natchez had 12 of them.

—Varina Buntin, a descendant of the Stantons, a prominent Natchez family

Whether or not that statement is precisely true, there's plenty of evidence to support the notion as you wander around Natchez. Try to time your Natchez visit with the Spring or Fall Pilgrimage, when you can take tours of the grand homes that now provide an economic lifeline to the city. Tours of the homes—which are still lived in—are conducted by the present owners, a charming group of people who are proud to open their dwellings and inform you of the buildings' histories. If you love antique furnishings, you should definitely take advantage of these tours.

If you find yourself in Natchez at an off-Pilgrimage time, you can still tour several historic homes, including the grandma of them all, **Stanton Hall,** maintained by the Pilgrimage Garden Club as its headquarters and as a historic house. Built in 1857 by Frederick Stanton, Stanton Hall is one of the region's most visited National

Historic Landmarks. Its scale is pleasantly overwhelming: the arched entry hall is 72 feet long, ceilings are 16.5 feet high, and the other rooms have similar proportions. The trees that grace the grounds of Stanton Hall's city block are century-old live oaks. Out back, the Carriage House Restaurant and Lounge specializes in Southern fried chicken and smashingly refreshing mint juleps.

Stanton Hall is one of Natchez's most stately historical mansions. Photo: F. Lynne Bachleda

Stanton Hall *401 High St. (at Pearl Street); 800-647-6742, stantonhall.com. Open daily, 9 a.m.–4:30 p.m. Admission is $20, with tours every half hour. Purchase tickets for the fall and spring private-home viewings through* **Natchez Pilgrimage Tours** *(60 S. Canal St.; 800-647-6742 or 601-446-6631, natchezpilgrimage.com). A three-house tour, which fills a leisurely morning, also costs $20. Other tour combinations are available.*

If you don't have time to do a Pilgrimage tour, make Melrose, part of Natchez National Historical Park and one of the original Pilgrimage homes, your one stop to understanding the scope and scale of local plantation life. In addition to the main house, Melrose's intact outbuildings include the kitchen, laundry, slave quarters, stable, and carriage house, plus a formal garden. Former slaves Jane Johnson and Alice Sims maintained the house during a long period when it was otherwise unoccupied.

The fee for the ranger-guided tour is $10 and must be paid by cash or check (National Parks Passes not accepted). Tours take about 45 minutes and are offered daily at 10 a.m., 11 a.m., 1 p.m., 2 p.m., 3 p.m., and 4 p.m. Admission to the grounds, outbuildings, and formal gardens is free.

Melrose Estate *Natchez National Historical Park, 1 Melrose–Montebello Parkway; 601-446-5790, nps.gov/natc. Open daily, 8:30 a.m.–5 p.m.*

Natchez is proof that geography is a powerful force. The city sits comfortably on a 200-foot bluff above the Mississippi River, a natural resource that helped bring the town to life and kept it thriving. Settled in 1716 by the French who established Fort Rosalie, Natchez is the oldest European-settled town on the river, beating New Orleans by two years. The area was inhabited, however, for centuries prior to the French by Mississippian Indians, known as Mound Builders, and their descendants, the Natchez. After the Natchez attacked Fort Rosalie, the French retaliated by decimating the tribe.

The Grand Hotel, near the Mississippi River in Natchez, is one of several fine accommodations in the city.

After France, Natchez came under the jurisdictions of England (1763), Spain (1779), and the United States (1795). Natchez was capital of the Mississippi Territory from 1798 to 1802. With the advent of the steamboat to export cotton, Natchez became a great river port and the cultural center of the planter aristocracy before the Civil War. Money flowed like the water in the river, and it funded stately mansions for the planter class. In *Life on the Mississippi,* Mark Twain remembered the city thus:

> *Natchez-on-top-of-the-Hill is attractive; has always been attractive. Even Mrs. Trollope (1827) had to confess its charms:*
>
> *"At one or two points the wearisome level line is relieved by bluffs, as they call the short intervals of high ground. The town of Natchez is beautifully situated on one of those high spots. The contrast that its bright green hill forms with the dismal line of black forest that stretches on every side, the abundant growth of the pawpaw, palmetto, and orange, the copious variety of sweet-scented flowers that flourish there, all make it appear like an oasis in the desert. . . ."*

Today Natchez relies in great part on tourists, who cannot resist the remains of its magnificence and romantic charm. It offers delightful eateries and accommodations, and since 2015 it has been home to **Magnolia Bluffs Casino and Hotel** (7 Roth Hill Road; 888-505-5777, 601-235-0045, magnoliabluffscasino.com), which brings in a large number of visitors to its riverside location just down the bluff from the **Natchez Grand Hotel** (111 Broadway St.; 866-488-0898, 601-446-9994, natchezgrandhotel.com).

THE NATCHEZ INDIANS

The Natchez tribe is the historical link to the Mound Builders of the Mississippi River Valley (extending from the Gulf of Mexico into Ohio), known for their flattop ceremonial mounds. It was the river that caused these several tribes, linked by Muskogean languages, to be called Mississippian.

At the time of the first European contact with Hernando de Soto in 1540, the Natchez, who had sketchy connections to de Soto, were a tribe numbering approximately 5,000 who lived in what is now the Natchez area. They inhabited present-day southwest Mississippi for about 1,000 years, from about AD 700 to 1730. **Grand Village** (see page 73), now a National Historic Landmark, was their religious and political center.

Farmers and hunters, the Natchez were noted for their fine hand-molded pottery and their fire-crafted canoes, which measured as much as 3 feet by 40 feet.

Encouraged by the English, who were enemies of France, the Natchez massacred the French at Fort Rosalie at dawn on November 28, 1729. French troops retaliated and, with the aid of Choctaw warriors, obliterated the tribe; of those who survived, some were sold into slavery in the British West Indies, while others fled and found refuge with the Cherokee, Creek, and Muscogee outside of Mississippi. Today the Natchez descended from these refugees live primarily in Oklahoma and South Carolina.

The Mississippi River at Natchez-Under-the-Hill

The basin of the Mississippi is the Body of the Nation. All the other parts are but members, important in themselves, yet more important in their relation to this.

—Mark Twain, *Life on the Mississippi*

"Father of Waters," as some American Indians called the Mississippi, is one of the longest rivers in the world. Its headwaters begin at Lake Itasca, Minnesota, where the river is 20–30 feet wide and about 3 feet deep. Heading south, the Mississippi merges and meanders for more than 2,300 miles until it empties into the Gulf of Mexico, about 60 miles southeast of New Orleans, at a depth of 200 feet.

Measurements of the river's length vary because the river is in a constant state of change. The Mississippi River is, however, the third-largest watershed in the world. Taking on the flow of the Missouri River in St. Louis, the Mississippi is the fourth-longest river in the world after the Nile, Amazon, and Yangtze.

Viewing the river at Natchez from near the bridge at the Natchez Visitor Center, you get a broad view of the Mississippi Delta's dirt drifting toward the Gulf. It's worth the drive across the bridge to the **Comfort Suites Vidalia** in Vidalia,

Louisiana (100 Front St.; 318-336-1655, tinyurl.com/comfortsuitesvidalia). Here you can enjoy a meal in the open air, take in a view of the Natchez bluff, and watch the weight of the world float by.

The Mississippi carries close to half a million pounds of sediment with it every day of the year. Some geologists think the waters of the Gulf of Mexico once reached as far north as Cairo, Illinois—meaning that over eons, the silting process may have created the land mass that is the south-central United States.

The Mississippi River transformed the Natchez Trace into an important highway home for the so-called Kaintuck boatmen who had floated their goods down to Natchez. The Trace unofficially begins at **Natchez–Under–the–Hill,** on the banks of the Mississippi—this is where the 19th-century flatboats and steamboats landed. Once a place of questionable repute where flatboat captains, flush with cash, flaunted their newfound riches on women and liquor, the area today is home to trendy gift shops and a few open-air restaurants. Natchez-Under-the-Hill is now a historic strip of buildings tucked under the bluff, easily accessible by car, so it's a good place to begin your journey.

The Mississippi River is hypnotizing. Watch it for 10 minutes, and you can sense its majesty and muscle. Essentially untamable, it is still prone to flooding. As Tennessee historian Ann Toplovich writes, "One of the world's natural wonders, the Mississippi River system looms large in the history and culture . . . and residents living along its banks continue to search for ways to live in harmony with its strength."

THE NATCHEZ SLAVE TRADE

Slaves! Slaves! Slaves! Forks of the Road, Natchez . . . just arrived . . . a choice selection of mechanics, field hands, cooks, washers and ironers, and general house servants.
            —November 27, 1858, *Natchez Daily Courier* advertisement

Traffic headed north on the Trace, mainly the Kaintuck boatmen, began to decline with the advent of the steamboat era in the early 1820s. But around the same time a new kind of traffic—enslaved humans—began traveling southeast on the Trace from Nashville to Natchez. Although in 1808 federal law prohibited importing Africans for the slave market, a steady stream of slaves arrived in the Chesapeake Bay area to toil on aging tobacco plantations. As demand for cotton by European textile mills began to eclipse that for tobacco, the need for slave labor began to weaken in Maryland and Virginia but grow stronger in the Deep South. In 1825–1830, for example, the average price in Virginia for a young male adult was $400. In Natchez, it was $560.

Natchez ranked only behind New Orleans in the trade of slaves. Its slave market was located at a crossroads just outside the city limits, called **Forks of the Road.**

Remembered now with a historical marker, Forks of the Road was then within sight of the grand mansions known today as Devereux, Linden, and Monmouth, all of which are often featured on Natchez Pilgrimage tours.

In the 1830s and early 1840s, Franklin & Armfield, then the leading slave-trading firm in the US, moved slaves overland on the Natchez Trace to Forks of the Road. During the 1830s they sent more than 1,000 slaves a year from their Alexandria, Virginia, headquarters to their Natchez and New Orleans markets.

The slave trade in Natchez came to a halt in 1863, when Union troops occupied the city that summer.

Forks of the Road was located at what is now the intersection of Liberty Road and St. Catherine Street/Devereux Drive in Natchez. **GPS: N31° 33.365' W91° 23.057'**

Grand Village of the Natchez Indians
ARCHAEOLOGY AND AMERICAN INDIANS

The Natchez mounds that survive today at Grand Village are, in a number of ways, like the cathedrals of Europe. They constructed consecrated spaces in stages, probably beginning in the 1200s AD—around the same time, in fact, that construction began on Chartres Cathedral in France. Grand Village was the center of life for the Natchez from at least 1682 until 1729, when the tribe provoked war with the French and was subsequently disbanded and dispersed.

At Grand Village you can observe a broad field and walk its circuit, studying at your leisure the reconstructed house and granary; a mound abandoned probably due to erosion from St. Catherine's Creek; the prehistoric and historic ceremonial plazas; the Great Sun's Mound; and the Temple Mound. Much more than just hills of dirt, these mounds hold the memories of many dramatic and sometimes deadly events.

While the great majority of the tribe lived on nearby farms, the chief, known as the Great Sun, lived at Grand Village on the prominent, centrally located mound. Here an inner sanctum housed the perpetual sacred fire, symbolic of the sun from which the royal family had descended. The Great Sun—who could be male or female—was worshipped as a living embodiment of the divine sun and held the power of life and death over other people. The Great Sun came to assume his or her position through matrilineal descent.

You can sit on the Great Sun's mound and empathize with the responsibilities of leadership, particularly the gravity of launching an attack on the ever-encroaching French—a decision that ultimately resulted in the loss of virtually everything and everyone, leaving only these mute mounds as witness.

Grand Village of the Natchez Indians *400 Jefferson Davis Blvd., Natchez; 660-446-6502 or tinyurl.com/natchezgrandvillage. Museum, gift shop, nature trails, and mound site. Open Monday–Saturday, 9 a.m.–5 p.m.; Sunday, 1:30–5 p.m. Free admission. In Natchez, turn east off US 61/South Sergeant Prentiss Drive onto Jefferson Davis Boulevard, just south of Natchez Regional Medical Center, and proceed on Jefferson Davis Boulevard 0.5 mile. The entrance gate is on the right.*

Between Natchez and Jackson

Long-range plans call for extending the Parkway into Natchez proper, probably designating the river landing at Natchez-Under-the-Hill as the official starting point. For now the **Natchez Visitor Center** serves as the de facto welcome station.

To find the visitor center, head toward the bridge (US 61/US 65/US 84) that spans the Mississippi into Vidalia, Louisiana. It's the modern building on the right, but access is from Canal Street (US 84), which runs parallel to the river on the bluff.

Natchez Visitor Center *640 S. Canal St.; 800-647-6724, visitnatchez.org. Open Monday–Saturday, 8:30 a.m.–5 p.m.; Sunday, 9 a.m.–4 p.m. Free exhibits, gift shop, and bookstore. You can watch a 20-minute film on Natchez history for a small fee.*

To get on the Natchez Trace Parkway, head north on US 61 until you see signs directing you right onto Liberty Road, which will connect you to the southern end of the Parkway. As you travel north on the Parkway, you'll come to **Elizabeth Female Academy,** on your left.

This is all that remains of Elizabeth Female Academy (1818–1845).

Milepost 5.1 Elizabeth Female Academy
✪ **TRACE TOP 20**

To reach this spot on the National Register of Historic Places, travel up to the milepost parking area, which then leads to a paved path to the ruins: an interior wall is all that remains of this distinguished school, which operated from 1818 to 1845.

Elizabeth Female Academy was the first degree-granting institution for women chartered in the state of Mississippi. Based on its advanced curriculum, some historians now argue that it was the very first women's college in the US, thus beating out Wesleyan College (1836) in Macon, Georgia, for the distinction. (At issue is whether the degree granted by the academy—*Domina Scientiarum,* or Mistress of Sciences—was the actual equivalent of a bachelor's degree.)

The academy represented progressive thinking as well as the needs of an emerging upper class that desired cultural refinements for their daughters. Varina Howell, who married the future president of the Confederacy, Jefferson Davis, was a graduate.

To extend this local tour of higher education, continue north a couple of miles to US 61. If you get off the Parkway here and travel south about 3 miles, you'll pass through **Washington,** Mississippi's first state capitol city, where you can visit **Historic Jefferson College.** Opened January 7, 1811, and named for the third president of the US, it was the first institution of higher learning in Mississippi. Noted naturalist John James Audubon taught at both Elizabeth Female Academy and Jefferson College in 1822 to 1823 while he recorded the birds of the Lower Mississippi region.

Historic Jefferson College *16 Old North St., Washington; 601-442-2901, historic jeffersoncollege.com. Buildings open Monday–Saturday, 9 a.m.–5 p.m.; Sunday, 1–5 p.m. Grounds open sunrise–sunset. Admission is free.*

Almost immediately after Jefferson College, you'll see the familiar brown signs directing you back onto the Parkway.

Milepost 8.7 Old Trace Exhibit Shelter
THE OLD TRACE

As you head north, this is your first glimpse at the Old Trace, so stop and take a look. Depending on the time of year and the thickness of the foliage, you can walk about 100 yards before the brush becomes forbidding in late spring. A small cemetery plot lies at the back of the field. This section gives you a sense of the sunken quality the old road sometimes has, having been worn down by animals over thousands of years. It also hints at an uneven surface that would have been most daunting and disabling to humans when extended over nearly 500 miles.

A section of the Old Trace leads into the woods at milepost 8.7. Photo: F. Lynne Bachleda

FRENCH, SPANISH, AND BRITISH PRESENCE

In 1541 the Spanish explorer Hernando de Soto and his men were the first Europeans to intrude upon the American Indians living along the Natchez Trace. Some 140 years later, French explorer Robert Cavelier, Sieur de la Salle, visited a Natchez tribal village, perhaps at Emerald Mound, during his adventures sailing down the

Mississippi River to its mouth at the Gulf of Mexico. Subsequently, he not so modestly claimed the entire Mississippi River Valley for France. In 1699 France's claim was reasserted by Pierre Le Moyne, Sieur d'Iberville, who established a trading relationship with the Natchez. The French strengthened their hold by building Fort Rosalie in present-day Natchez on the grounds of what later became Rosalie Mansion.

The Natchez rebelled at the increasing French presence by attacking the fort, killing 250 men, and taking 300 women and children as prisoners. Within weeks the French retaliated and destroyed the Natchez tribe, the first group to suffer enormous losses at the hands of the Europeans. Eager to assert themselves farther into the region, the French led an attack on the Chickasaw six years later, in 1736, near the village of Ackia. They were joined by the Choctaw, traditional enemies of the Chickasaw, but with some support from the British in the form of supplies, the Chickasaw soundly defeated the invaders, and France's importance in the region began to wane.

In the first Treaty of Paris, in 1763, England claimed France's possessions east of the Mississippi. The English rebuilt Fort Rosalie, renaming it Fort Panmure, and held the region as British West Florida until Spain reappeared on the Gulf Coast and occupied Natchez until the late 1790s.

The Second Treaty of Paris, signed in 1783 by England and the United States, acknowledged America's claim to the West Florida Territory south to the 31st Parallel. Spain objected, insisting that the US's claim stopped slightly north, at N32° 28.000´. The dispute continued until 1795, when Spain finally accepted the more southern boundary. With Spain's eventual withdrawal from the area in 1798, when the Mississippi Territory was organized, the last European claim to the Natchez Trace region ended. The first European nation to arrive was the last to leave, but even after the territory came under the control of the fledgling United States, the impact of various European cultures lingered for many years.

Milepost 10.3 Emerald Mound
✪ TRACE TOP 20, ARCHAEOLOGY AND AMERICAN INDIANS

If you're impressed by scale, you'll love Emerald Mound. Named for Emerald Plantation, whose acreage once encompassed it, the mound staggers the imagination with its scale when you contemplate its construction. The nation's second-largest Mississippian structure, Emerald Mound covers nearly 8 acres and is superseded only by Monk's Mound at Cahokia, Illinois. It measures 770 feet by 435 feet at its base (roughly 2.5 by 1.5 football fields) and is approximately 35 feet high. A steep paved path leads to the first plateau.

Covering roughly 8 acres, Emerald Mound is mind-boggling in size.

Ancestors of the Natchez built and used this ceremonial mound from about AD 1250–1600. After that time, and for reasons unknown, the Mississippian Indians who built it shifted their ceremonial center to Grand Village. A subject of archaeological investigations beginning in 1838, the mound was built by depositing earth along the sides of a natural hill. When you consider that southern Mississippi isn't exactly hill country, the scope of the labor and intent to build Emerald Mound begins to take shape.

On top of the main, large plateau, you'll find two more mounds at either end, both impressive as stand-alone structures. The larger one measures 190 by 160 feet at its base and 30 feet tall, which puts you at about treetop-high. Early drawings suggest that there may also have been four or six smaller mounds along the edges. When you approach and ascend Emerald Mound, you're on consecrated ground where elaborate civic processions, ceremonial dances, and intricate and solemn religious rituals were conducted.

Reach Emerald Mound by exiting the Parkway at milepost 10.3, at the MS 553 intersection. Follow the signs about 1 mile (about 3 minutes) along a rural road.
GPS: N31° 38.125' W91° 14.859'

Milepost 12.1 Turpin Creek
NATURAL WONDERS

A picnic area is located alongside the road. The creek here isn't as interesting as at other creekside picnic areas, but several tables and grills are available.

Milepost 12.4 Loess Bluff
NATURAL WONDERS

What at first appears to be a nondescript exposed hillside is actually a glimpse into a geological process that began during the Pleistocene epoch, 1 million years ago. Deposits of silt, or *loess,* (pronounced "Lois") were blown here from the north during the last ice age. Thick loess deposits such as this are generally found in areas where there were glaciers. As glaciers melted in the summer months, finely ground water-borne sediment formed at the edges of the glaciers. In winter, when the water stopped flowing, the winter winds carried this fine sediment in huge dust storms. As the wind died down, the silt fell to the earth, creating deposits such as the one you see here. Loess deposits are frequently most extensive and thickest downwind from large river valleys (and the Mississippi River Valley certainly is one).

Milepost 15.5 Mount Locust Historic Inn and Plantation
✪ TRACE TOP 20, KAINTUCK BOATMEN AND THE POSTAL ROAD

Of the 50 or so roadside hostelries established before 1820 along the Trace, only Mount Locust remains. It is one of the oldest buildings in Mississippi, dating to 1780. In 1956 it was restored to its form as a plantation home of the 1820s, which was the peak era of the Trace's foot and horse travel. Food and accommodations cost about 25¢ per night.

The home is furnished with period belongings, and a quick hike behind the house leads to a slave cemetery that holds the resting places of 43 people; a marker lists the names of the deceased. The core of the house was built by Swiss-born John Blommart before it was acquired by his business associate, William Ferguson,

Mount Locust's rooms are furnished with period pieces that give visitors a glimpse at life on the Trace.

Mount Locust is one of about 50 inns that operated along the Trace before 1820.

who eventually increased his holdings to 1,215 acres and many slaves.

While planting was Ferguson's major interest, he also attempted to create a thriving village called Uniontown, which was to occupy the land in front of Mount Locust. The main street of Uniontown is still visible running parallel near the Trace. The town, which had about half a dozen buildings, began to decline after it was rejected as the county seat and after Ferguson's death in 1801.

Ferguson's widow, Paulina, subsequently married James Chamberlain. Mount Locust Inn and Plantation prospered as the Trace traffic grew, for Mount Locust was a one-day walk from Natchez. Andrew Jackson reportedly stayed here twice. Among its many outbuildings is a four-room, two-story annex called Sleepy Hollow, built to hold wall-to-wall corn shuck mattresses.

After her husband abandoned her in 1810, Paulina Ferguson carried on nobly and industriously. When she died in 1849, Mount Locust was appraised at around $50,000; her heirs thrived as cotton planters before the Civil War. Thomas Jefferson Chamberlain, her son, was a wealthy man when he died, owning more than 100 enslaved African Americans. Many of these slaves joined the Union army during the war, fighting as United States Colored Troops before returning to work as sharecroppers after the war, some at Mount Locust.

Milepost 17.0 Potkopinu Trail: Southern Section
THE OLD TRACE

The trailhead to this newly recovered section of the Old Trace is just east of the Parkway on Geoghegan Road, near milepost 17.0 (**GPS: 31° 42.193' W91° 10.705'**). Part of the Natchez Trace National Scenic Trail (see page 51), it has stunning, pristine beauty, as does the section described on the next page near milepost 20.0. This 3-mile trail is the longest remaining stretch of the so-called Sunken Trace. In some cases, embankments are more than 20 feet high. The trailhead is not recommended for RVs; check with the Parkway Visitor Center (800-305-7417) or visit nps.gov/natt to confirm conditions.

Milepost 17.5 Coles Creek
NATURAL WONDERS

This stop has a picnic area with around 20 creekside tables and restrooms.

Milepost 18.4 Bullen Creek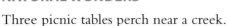
NATURAL WONDERS

The Parkway offers numerous opportunities for a simple, relatively short leg stretch. At Bullen Creek a flat, self-guided trail leads through a mixed hardwood–pine forest. The walk takes 15 minutes at a leisurely stroll.

Milepost 20.0 Potkopinu Trail: Northern Section
THE OLD TRACE

The trailhead to this newly recovered section of the Old Trace is 1 mile east of the Parkway on MS 553 (**GPS: N31° 44.708' W91° 09.336'**). Part of the Natchez Trace National Scenic Trail (see page 51), it has stunning, pristine beauty, as does the section described on the previous page near milepost 17.0. This trailhead accommodates RVs, but check with the Parkway Visitor Center (800-305-7417) or visit nps.gov/natt to confirm conditions.

Milepost 22.0 Mud Island Creek
NATURAL WONDERS

Three picnic tables perch near a creek.

Milepost 23.0 North Fork Coles Creek
NATURAL WONDERS

A sizable field and a few picnic tables mark this spot where you can see the creek through the trees.

Milepost 30.0 Windsor Ruins
KAINTUCK BOATMEN AND THE POSTAL ROAD, THE LIVING TRACE

Note: Allot 45 minutes to an hour or more for this side trip off the Parkway.

One of the most visually stunning detours off the Parkway takes you to the ghostly form of an antebellum mansion. Windsor was built by Smith Coffee Daniell II—begun in 1859 and finished in 1861—just before the Civil War

Spooky Southern grandeur awaits at the Windsor Ruins. Photo: F. Lynne Bachleda

began. Tragically, Daniell, who was only 34, died just a few weeks after its completion. The total cost of the mansion was $175,000, or more than $3 million by today's numbers.

At its peak the entire Windsor plantation sprawled over 2,600 acres. The four-story home had 25 rooms with 25 fireplaces, and attic tanks supplied water to the interior baths. The basement floor had a schoolroom, dairy, and supply rooms. The roof observatory was used to signal Confederate troops about Union advances. Twenty-nine 45-foot-tall columns were joined across the front with an ornamental iron balustrade. Windsor was used as a Union hospital during the Civil War and survived intact.

In an ironic turn of events, however, on February 17, 1890, a fire broke out after a party guest accidentally dropped a cigarette on the third floor. Windsor burned to the ground, leaving only a few pieces of china, 23 columns, and the balustrade. The ruins were immortalized in two films: *Raintree County* (1957), starring Elizabeth Taylor and Montgomery Clift, and *Ghosts of Mississippi* (1996), starring Whoopi Goldberg, Alec Baldwin, and James Woods.

Visiting the Windsor Ruins today is an eerily beautiful experience. The scale of the columns points clearly to a former grandeur that the powers of fire, earth, and time have since reclaimed as their own.

Windsor Ruins *Rodney Road, about 3 miles north of Alcorn State University; 601-576-6952, mdah.ms.gov/new/visit/windsor-ruins. Open daily, sunrise–sunset; admission is free. Heading north on the Parkway, exit onto MS 552 at milepost 30.0, and follow the signs west and then north about 11 miles. The ruins are on the right (east) side of the road (*GPS: N31° 56.436' W91° 07.770'*). You can also access them farther north on the Parkway, off milepost 41.0 (see next page).*

From Port Gibson, about 10.4 miles east of the Windsor Ruins on Rodney Road, you can get back on the Parkway or head north on US 61 to **Vicksburg National Military Park** (see below). To return to the Parkway, go north (left) on US 61 and, at the intersection with MS 18, go right. In 1 mile head right (north) on the Parkway toward Jackson.

Milepost 38.0 Vicksburg National Military Park
CIVIL WAR AND OTHER MILITARY HISTORY
    Note: *Allot at least 2 hours for this side trip.*

The Vicksburg campaign was waged March 29–July 4, 1863. It included battles in west-central Mississippi at Port Gibson, Raymond, Jackson, Champion Hill, and Big Black River, as well as 47 days of Union siege operations against Confederate forces defending the city of Vicksburg.

Located high on the bluffs, Vicksburg was a fortress guarding the Mississippi River (its nickname was "The Gibraltar of the Confederacy"). Its surrender on July 4, 1863, coupled with the fall of Port Hudson, Louisiana, divided the South and gave the North undisputed control of the Mississippi River.

Today, the battlefield at Vicksburg is in an excellent state of preservation. It includes more than 1,400 historic monuments and markers, 20 miles of reconstructed trenches and earthworks, a 16-mile tour road, an antebellum home, 144 emplaced cannon, the restored Union gunboat USS *Cairo,* and Vicksburg National Cemetery.

Vicksburg National Military Park *3201 Clay St., Vicksburg; 601-636-2199 or 601-636-0583, nps.gov/vick. Open daily except Thanksgiving, December 25, and January 1; admission is $20 per vehicle (National Parks Passes accepted). Visitor Center open 8 a.m.– 5 p.m.; USS* Cairo *Gunboat and Museum open 8:30 a.m.–5 p.m. Heading north on the Parkway, exit onto MS 61 North at milepost 38.0 and, in about 26 miles, merge onto I-20 East. In 3.8 miles, take Exit 4B onto West Clay Street, and in 0.6 mile turn right onto Union Avenue to reach the parking area.*

Milepost 41.0 Windsor Ruins
KAINTUCK BOATMEN AND THE POSTAL ROAD, THE LIVING TRACE

(See description at milepost 300.) From the southbound Parkway exit at milepost 41.0 in Port Gibson, head west 1.1 miles on MS 18; turn left (south) onto US 61 and, in 0.7 mile, turn right (west) onto Carroll Street, which becomes Rodney Road. The ruins are 10.2 miles ahead on the left (east) side of the road.
GPS: N31° 56.436' W91° 07.770'

Milepost 41.5 The Sunken Trace
THE OLD TRACE

This short but compelling section of the Old Trace will open your imagination. Animals first wore down this path, then people. In fading sunlight, within these high earthen walls, it's easy to picture how easily outlaws could ambushed the unsuspecting along the Trace. On this section of the Trace, you're looking at the effects of time, hooves, and feet. The trail

Worn by time and the traffic of humans and animals, the Sunken Trace shows what travelers experienced before the advent of motor vehicles.

is very short, and the NPS recommends 5 minutes here, but if you linger a bit, you may sense the spirit of those who trod here before you.

Milepost 45.7 Grindstone Ford and Mangum Mound
ARCHAEOLOGY AND AMERICAN INDIANS, KAINTUCK BOATMEN AND THE POSTAL ROAD

After pulling off the Parkway, you come to a parking lot that doesn't lead to either Grindstone Ford or Mangum Mound—instead, you pass through the lot to arrive at an intersection where you can turn left toward the mound or right toward the ford.

The main attraction of Grindstone Ford is a short, flat loop trail that leads to one of seven historical cemeteries along the Parkway. Northbound travelers believed they were entering wild country when they crossed Grindstone Ford on Bayou Pierre, about 45 miles, or a two-day walk, from Natchez. In fact, they were entering the Choctaw Nation. Grindstone Ford was named for a water-driven mill nearby. This was a substantial water-crossing landmark, as Bayou Pierre can be floated for more than 100 miles before it eventually feeds into the Mississippi River.

Mangum Mound, a subtle rise, is a remnant from the Plaquemine Indian culture, which flourished about AD 1000 and was a forerunner of the Natchez civilization. To reach it, you travel through a farm and pasture, but be aware that the mound is some-

Not as well defined as many of the ancient mounds on the Trace, Mangum Mound sits amid farmland and private property.

what hard to identify in its current context. The Plaquemine often built mounds on top of the ruins of a house or temple, constructing similar buildings on top of the mound using wattle and daub (interwoven rods and laths or twigs plastered with mud or clay), sometimes with wall posts sunk into foot-deep wall trenches. These Indians also dug shallow graves in the mounds, intended primarily for the reburial of remains originally interred elsewhere.

Owens Creek Falls flows faintly except after heavy rains. Photo: F. Lynne Bachleda

Milepost 52.4 Owens Creek Falls

NATURAL WONDERS

The flow here is just a trickle unless it has recently rained heavily, but you can still relax and enjoy a bite to eat at the picnic table. *Note:* A spur trail to the falls and the 2.5-mile trail to Rocky Springs (see below) are closed at the time of this writing due to safety concerns. Please obey all posted closure signs.

Milepost 54.8 Rocky Springs

☼ TRACE TOP 20, THE LIVING TRACE, THE OLD TRACE, NPS INFORMATION

This site offers a 22-site campground, a 7-mile hiking trail, and the remnants of a ghost town. Follow the paved road through several parking areas, the farthest of which is the trailhead leading to the old village of Rocky Springs. This short, easy loop leads past two old safes and on to an 1837 church, still in occasional use, and its cemetery, both of which are on private property yet are open to the public. An old tree with exposed roots rises in front of the church, which is still used for occasional Sunday services and can be rented for weddings or other occasions. The church, cemetery, and flora are a photographer's delight.

Two hundred years ago, Rocky Springs was a thriving little town whose settlement began in the 1790s and grew to several thousand at its peak in the 1850s.

Rocky Springs Church is still used for church services and weddings.
Photo: F. Lynne Bachleda

This is somewhat hard to imagine as you walk a short section of the Old Trace where the chief activity is the growth of grass underfoot—the homes, school, post office, and Masonic lodge that once were here are all gone. Occupation by General Ulysses S. Grant's 40,000 Union troops in 1863, a yellow fever outbreak in 1878, a boll weevil infestation in the early 1900s, and the death of the spring itself sealed Rocky Springs' fate. See Chapter 2, "The Nuts and Bolts of Traveling the Trace" (page 28), for more information on the campground here.

THE CHOCTAW NATION

Like the Natchez, the Choctaw are linked to the Mississippian Mound Builder culture, but the link is not as obvious or as certain—if the Choctaw did build mounds, they had long ceased to build them by the time of white settlement. Still, the central legend of the Choctaw is that they originated from Nanih Waiya, a sacred hill near what is now Noxapater, Mississippi. *Nanih Waiya* means "productive mound" and is often referred to as The Mother Mound. (Women in Choctaw culture have always been honored as the head of every household.)

The Choctaw were considered the best farmers of the Indians in the Southeast, growing enough food to be able to barter with it. They shared many cultural practices with their neighbors, the Natchez.

The Choctaw had several wars with the Chickasaw, their neighbors to the north, but they also brokered several effective peace treaties. Some scholars think the two tribes may have been one long ago; early writers mention a "hereditary" enmity between the two. The rivalry between the Choctaw and the Chickasaw may also have been aggravated by the onslaught of Europeans, who sought to divide and conquer.

The relationship between the Choctaw and white settlers was complex. Chief Pushmataha, affirming his allegiance to the United States, led several hundred warriors with Andrew Jackson at the Battles of New Orleans and Horseshoe Bend (Alabama). But the Choctaw were the first of the five great Southeastern US tribes to be moved to Oklahoma by the Treaty of Dancing Rabbit Creek in 1830. More than 20,000 Choctaw were forced to make this long, arduous journey. Many did not survive, which is why the trip is often referred to as the Trail of Tears. Although historically associated with the Cherokee, the Trail of Tears has come to represent the removal and relocation of all Southeastern Indian tribes.

During World War II, Choctaw code talkers relied upon their linguistic heritage to create unbreakable codes. Today's Choctaw live in their ancestral homelands in Mississippi as well as in Oklahoma, where the so-called Western Band reestablished a thriving culture.

Milepost 61.0 Lower Choctaw Boundary
ARCHAEOLOGY AND AMERICAN INDIANS

A line of trees marks the southern boundary of the Choctaw Nation as well as the line between Hinds and Claiborne Counties. It also marked the spot of Red Bluff Stand; owned by John Gregg and established in 1802, it was the last white-owned hostelry and supply station on the northbound Trace before one entered Choctaw territory.

Milepost 73.5 Dean Stand 🏕
KAINTUCK BOATMEN AND THE POSTAL ROAD, THE OLD TRACE

This point of interest is easy to miss, as it's not directly on the Parkway and the road that takes you 0.1 mile to the parking lot and picnic area has no signage.
GPS: N32° 14.057' W90° 32.460'

Milepost 78.3 Battle of Raymond 🏕
CIVIL WAR AND OTHER MILITARY HISTORY

Near this site on Tuesday, May 12, 1863, Confederate brigade forces commanded by Brigadier General John Gregg attacked the Union division, part of Ulysses Grant's forces led by Major General John A. Logan. The Confederates were driven back toward Jackson, Mississippi, after several hours of fighting. About 1,000 men were killed or wounded, in a loss borne equally by the Union and the Confederacy.

Jackson

Beautiful and healthful surroundings, good water, abundant timber, navigable waters, and nearness to the Natchez Trace . . .

—From an 1821 report to the Mississippi General Assembly recommending Jackson as the new state capital

The city of Jackson began as a trading post known as LeFleur's Bluff, named for French Canadian trader Louis LeFleur. Situated on a high bluff of the Pearl River, Jackson—named for the seventh president—was established in 1821 as the site of the new capital of Mississippi. Affairs of state subsequently moved here from the old capital of Natchez.

Jackson was burned three times during the Civil War by General William Tecumseh Sherman's Union troops. City Hall, built in 1846 and still in use today, was probably spared the torch because it was serving as a hospital.

The Jackson metropolitan area (population: 580,000) supports various museums and cultural institutions, as well as historical sites pertaining to the Civil War era and the 1960s struggle for civil rights.

For detailed information on attractions and lodging in Jackson, contact the **Jackson Convention and Visitors Bureau** (111 E. Capitol St., Ste. 102; 800-354-7695, visitjackson.com).

Milepost 88.1 Cowles Mead Cemetery
THE LIVING TRACE

Cowles Mead (1776–1844), a Georgia native who owned a tavern on the Trace near Natchez, also held several political offices. As acting governor in 1806, he ordered the arrest for treason of former vice president Aaron Burr, who was later acquitted. As the city of Jackson grew, Meade moved farther out and built a home, Greenwood, at this site. It burned during the Civil War, and now only a family burial plot remains with the graves of Mead and his wife, Mary. A short paved path takes you to the cemetery.

Cowles Mead Cemetery is the resting place of its namesake and his wife.

Milepost 93.1 Osburn Stand
KAINTUCK BOATMEN AND THE POSTAL ROAD

Beginning in 1806, the Choctaw allowed inns, or stands, to be constructed along the Trace. By 1811 a man named Noble Osburn operated a stand here to provide food and shelter for Trace travelers. He had a reputation for treating whites and Indians equally. There's nothing to see here today, however, but an informational panel.

Milepost 100.7 Choctaw Agency
ARCHAEOLOGY AND AMERICAN INDIANS

From 1807 until 1820, Silas Dinsmore lived at this site while holding the difficult job of Choctaw agent. His responsibilities included representing the interests of the Choctaw while implementing US policies. He checked passports, collected debts, and ensured that the Choctaw were paid for lands ceded to the United States. He also taught farming methods to the Choctaw. As tribal lands continued to shrink in the face of pioneer settlement demands, the Choctaw Agency had to move four times to remain within tribal boundaries.

Trace Tip

The Choctaw Agency stop also offers access and parking for the **Chisha Foka Multi-Use Trail** (see page 49).

Milepost 102.4 Parkway Information Cabin
NPS INFORMATION

The first interpretive center on the Parkway in 1951, this dogtrot-style cabin was reopened in September 2009 as an NPS seasonal-information center. It offers information and interpretive programs about the Natchez Trace, brochures on area attractions, a picnic area, and an Eastern National store that sells Trace-related books and gifts. The **Mississippi Crafts Center** (950 Rice Road; 601-856-7546, craftsmensguildofms.org) was headquartered here from 1975 to 2007 but is now 3 miles north; signs on the Parkway will direct you to it.

Between Jackson and Tupelo

Milepost 104.5 Old Trace and Brashears Stand Site
KAINTUCK BOATMEN AND THE POSTAL ROAD, THE OLD TRACE

The first inn allowed by the Choctaw Nation was Turner Brashears's stand, advertised to travelers as "a house of entertainment in the wilderness" when it opened in 1806. A short section of the original Trace is nearby. A new trail and boardwalk connect this Parkway stop to the **Mississippi Crafts Center** (see above); the site also serves as a parking/access point for the **Chisha Foka Multi-Use Trail** (see page 49).

Milepost 105.6 Ross R. Barnett Reservoir Overlook
✪ TRACE TOP 20, NATURAL WONDERS

Created by impounding the Pearl River between Madison and Rankin Counties, the 33,000-acre Ross R. Barnett Reservoir parallels the Parkway for 8 miles. Bound by the Natchez Trace on the north, it has 105 miles of shoreline. The reservoir is named for Ross R. Barnett (1898–1987), governor of Mississippi from 1960 to 1966.

The Pearl River Valley Water Supply District, which administers the reservoir, provides recreational opportunities in the

Ross R. Barnett Reservoir covers 33,000 acres and spans two Mississippi counties. Photo: F. Lynne Bachleda

area: 48 parks and outdoor facilities, including 5 campgrounds, 16 parks, 22 boat launches, 3 wheelchair-accessible trails, 2 multipurpose trails, and a mountain bike trail. Each campground has a live-in, on-site reservoir patrol manager. In conjunction with the private and public sectors, the water-supply district has also developed five marinas, four baseball and soccer complexes, two golf courses, and a water park.

Trace Tip

A $5 traffic-control fee may be collected at the reservoir on weekends and holidays during months of heavy use.

The reservoir offers numerous places to launch a boat and paddle. The official map, which lists all boat ramps, depth contours, structures, fishing information, and GPS points, covers the reservoir and the Pearl River from the spillway north to Tuscolameta Creek, just upriver from the MS 25 bridge. For more information, go to therez.ms.gov/pages/parks-recreation.aspx.

Milepost 106.9 Boyd Site
ARCHAEOLOGY AND AMERICAN INDIANS

Most known burial mounds in Mississippi date to the Middle Woodland period (circa 100 BC–AD 400). The six small burial mounds at the Boyd Site, however, were built much later, during the Late Woodland and Early Mississippian periods, circa AD 800–1100. One of these, Mound 2, is accessible to visitors.

Several of the mounds, including Mound 2, were excavated by the NPS in 1964. The elongated Mound 2 is 110 feet long by 60 feet wide and 4 feet high. Excavation revealed that it is actually three mounds in one: initially, two mounds were built side by side, then both were covered with more earth to create a single oblong mound. The remains of 41 individuals were found in Mound 2, but there were few accompanying artifacts. Different pottery types found in separate areas of this compound mound indicate that it was constructed in two phases: first during the Late Woodland period and then, after a considerable length of time, during the Mississippian period.

Milepost 107.9 West Florida Boundary
THE LIVING TRACE

In 1764 this spot was the northern boundary of the West Florida Territory, marked by a line from the Yazoo and Mississippi Rivers' confluence east to the Chattahoochee River. Today it's the southern trailhead for the 25-mile Yockanookany Trail, part of the Natchez Trace National Scenic Trail (see page 51).

Milepost 122.0 Cypress Swamp ⬦ TRACE TOP 20, NATURAL WONDERS

Crossing the wooden footbridge into this swamp, you enter a watery, quiet world populated primarily by water tupelo and bald cypress. You can enjoy this easy, flat walking trail in 15 minutes, or you can savor it for much longer, quietly waiting for swamp wildlife such as herons and alligators to appear. The tranquility here can be hypnotic if you take your time.

Water tupelos (*Nyssa aquatica*) have a bulbous base and grow to a mature height of 90 feet, with a spread of 30 feet. Their foliage turns orange-red in the fall, and small, clustered, greenish-white flowers appear in spring with the new leaves. The tree's fruit is 1 inch long, pear-shaped, and reddish purple in color.

Mature bald cypress (*Taxodium distichum*) grows to a height of 70 feet, with a 30-foot spread. Contrary to popular belief, this deciduous conifer can grow in a variety of soils—even dry, compacted ones—but it must have water to

This cypress swamp has an unearthly Southern Gothic feel. Photo: F. Lynne Bachleda

germinate, hence its association with swamplands. In swamps the trees form "knees," stubby growths that help aerate the plant as well as provide stability in high winds. Bald cypresses have even been known to survive hurricanes.

Milepost 122.6 River Bend
NATURAL WONDERS

This lovely picnic spot has 29 picnic tables, 15 grills, and restrooms. The Pearl River, named by French explorer Pierre Le Moyne, Sieur d'Iberville, for the many native pearls he found here, is the focus of this scenic area. The river marks a boundary between Mississippi and Louisiana.

Milepost 128.4 Upper Choctaw Boundary
ARCHAEOLOGY AND AMERICAN INDIANS, NATURAL WONDERS

This short nature loop through Southern pines is an easy 10-minute walk. A line of trees that now blends into the surrounding growth marks the dividing line established at the Treaty of Doaks Stand on October 20, 1820. As a condition of this treaty, the Choctaw surrendered one-third of their tribal land—millions of acres—to the United States. Within 10 years of signing the treaty, the Choctaw no longer held claim to any land east of the Mississippi.

Milepost 130.9 Yockanookany
NATURAL WONDERS

This is the northern trailhead for the Yockanookany Trail, part of the Natchez Trace National Scenic Trail (see page 51). The Yockanookany River is nearby. (*Yockanookany* is a Choctaw word meaning "has been lost.")

Milepost 135.5 Robinson Road
KAINTUCK BOATMEN AND THE POSTAL ROAD

Now on the National Register of Historic Places, Robinson Road was begun in 1821 and became a major thoroughfare for travel between Jackson and Columbus. A picnic table and informational panel mark the site.

Milepost 140.0 Red Dog Road
ARCHAEOLOGY AND AMERICAN INDIANS

An informational panel describes this Trace crossroad. Named for Choctaw *minko* (leader) Ofahoma ("Red Dog" in English) and opened in 1834, the road originated in Canton, Mississippi.

Milepost 145.1 Myrick Creek
NATURAL WONDERS

Stretch your legs on this pleasant, flat, 5- to 10-minute walk. A shelter has informational panels.

Milepost 154.3 Holly Hill
NATURAL WONDERS

Here you'll find a restroom and picnic area, including one table accessible to people with disabilities.

Milepost 160.0 Kosciusko Welcome Center
THE LIVING TRACE

Volunteers with the Kosciusko–Attala Partnership provide travel information for both the Parkway and the surrounding area in this small, comfortable visitor center, which also offers nature and history exhibits and restrooms. Adjacent to the main building is one of the few bicycle-only campgrounds along the Parkway (see page 148).

Kosciusko Welcome Center *Just north of the Parkway and east of MS 35, Kosciusko; 662-289-2981. Open daily, 9 a.m.–5 p.m.*

IN SEARCH OF OPRAH

One of the most famous and influential people in the world was born January 29, 1954, in a long-demolished farmhouse on the rural outskirts of Kosciusko, not far from the Natchez Trace Parkway. Her name on her birth certificate was Orpah Gail Winfrey (Orpah being a figure from the Old Testament), but so many people called her Oprah that the mispronunciation (and misspelling) stuck.

Winfrey started her broadcasting career in Nashville at radio station WVOL while she was still in high school. At the age of 19, she became both the youngest person and the first African American woman to anchor the news at Nashville's WTVF-TV.

The Oprah Winfrey Show, which aired from 1986 to 2011, received so many Emmys (47 in all) that Winfrey withdrew it from future competition in 2000. She made her acting debut in 1985 as Sofia in the film adaptation of Alice Walker's *The Color Purple,* a role for which she received both Oscar and Golden Globe nominations. In 2009 she launched her own cable channel, the Oprah Winfrey Network (OWN).

By her 40s Winfrey headed a multimedia empire encompassing TV and film production as well as a magazine and website. She is a renowned philanthropist, and her book-club initiative has propelled many of its featured selections to the best-seller lists. She was an early supporter of Barack Obama's 2008 presidential campaign and has provoked speculation more recently about a presidential bid of her own (she has publicly denied that she's interested). And she continues to act, having most recently costarred in the Disney adaptation of Madeleine L'Engle's *A Wrinkle in Time* (2018).

Time magazine named Winfrey as one of its 100 Most Influential People of the 20th Century, and she was the only living person to make *Life* magazine's list of 100 People Who Changed the World. In 1999 she was recognized for championing reading and literature when she received the National Book Foundation's 50th Anniversary Gold Medal. In 2002 she was the first recipient of the Bob Hope Humanitarian Award, and in 2013 she was awarded the Presidential Medal of Freedom.

Winfrey lived the first six years of her life near Kosciusko. To see the sites marking her humble origins, exit the Parkway at milepost 160.0 onto northbound MS 35. In about 2.4 miles, turn right (east) onto MS 12. About 2.7 miles farther, Oprah Winfrey Road (formerly Buffalo Road) makes a loop off the left (north) side of MS 12. Before you return to the highway, you'll pass Winfrey's childhood church (now the **Buffalo Community Center**), her family cemetery, and the site of her birthplace.

Milepost 164.3 Hurricane Creek
NATURAL WONDERS

Allow 10 minutes to walk this easy trail with a slight elevation gain. Begin by descending into bottomland along the creek banks; then ascend to a more-arid zone that supports different tree and plant species from those of the wetter lower elevation. A bench at the top of the trail rewards you with a place to rest before you head back. Self-guiding trail markers identify plants and different soil conditions.

Milepost 175.6 Cole Creek
NATURAL WONDERS

This short, self-guiding, 10-minute trail commences with a charming wooden footbridge and leads you through a tupelo–bald cypress swamp that is evolving into a mixed-hardwood forest. This natural evolutionary process, which takes hundreds of years to complete, involves the very gradual leveling of the land. Eventually the changed landscape adapts to support vegetation that needs only moderate water, replacing plants that thrive in very moist or very arid soil.

Milepost 176.3 Bethel Mission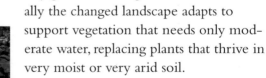
ARCHAEOLOGY AND AMERICAN INDIANS, NATURAL WONDERS

For five years, from 1821 until it closed in 1826 as traffic moved away from the Trace, the Bethel (aka House of God) Mission

A variety of vegetation grows in the Trace's different riparian zones.

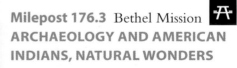

On the trail at Jeff Busby Park Photo: Michael Gaylard/
CC BY 2.0 (creativecommons.org/licenses/by-2.0)

level. Exhibits at the crest tell the story of America's forests. Because the trail winds and rises—allow for 30 minutes of hiking time unless you're in attack mode—some travelers may wish to drive to the top to enjoy the view. In addition to the trail, restrooms, and a picnic area, Jeff Busby Park has what is regarded as one of the better campgrounds along the Parkway (see page 148).

Thomas Jefferson "Jeff" Busby (1884–1964), a former schoolteacher and county prosecutor who served as a US Representative from 1923 to 1935, is honored at this central location on the Parkway. The honor is fitting: it was Busby who shepherded a measure through Congress in the mid-1930s "to locate the Natchez Trace as near as practical in its original route and to determine the cost of construction of an appropriate National Parkway."

Milepost 198.6 Old Trace
THE OLD TRACE

Walking this broad section of the Old Trace, you get a distinct understanding of how it meanders across and alongside the present Parkway. Wear closed-toed shoes and probably long pants to protect you from poison ivy and other itchies, such as chiggers, to enjoy this out-and-back section of the original roadway, which leads approximately 500 yards into the woods.

Milepost 201.3 Ballard Creek
NATURAL WONDERS

This stop has a fairly secluded picnic area with one table.

Milepost 203.5 Pigeon Roost
KAINTUCK BOATMEN AND THE POSTAL ROAD, NATURAL WONDERS

Folsom's Stand and Trading Post, operated by Nathaniel and David Folsom, once stood near this point. Millions of passenger pigeons, now extinct, also once roosted here.

Milepost 213.3 Line Creek
ARCHAEOLOGY AND AMERICAN INDIANS

This stop consists of a picnic table and an informational panel that describes the creek's onetime function as a border between Choctaw and Chickasaw lands.

Milepost 221.4 Old Trace
THE OLD TRACE

This approximately 10-foot-wide section of the Old Trace crosses the Parkway. The excursion, about 20 minutes out-and-back, is another opportunity to walk in the footsteps of previous Natchez Trace travelers. Closed-toed shoes are a must.

Milepost 232.4 Bynum Mounds
ARCHAEOLOGY AND AMERICAN INDIANS

A paved path leads around two of six burial mounds found here and believed to have been built during the Middle Woodland period, between 100 BC and AD 100. The mounds range from 5 to 14 feet tall; the NPS excavated five of them in the late 1940s.

Mound A, the southernmost of the two restored mounds, contained the remains of a woman who was buried between two burned oak logs laid at a parallel at the mound's base. She was buried with an ornamental copper spool at each wrist. The cremated traces of two adults and a child were also found here.

Mound B, the largest at the site, covered a log-lined crematory pit. An L-shaped row of 29 polished greenstone celts (ax heads) and the cremated and unburned remains of several individuals were found on the ash-covered floor.

A walking path winds through the Bynum Mounds. Photo: F. Lynne Bachleda

Other artifacts found laid in ceremonial context include copper spools, 19 chert projectile points from Illinois, and a piece of galena (lead ore). Greenstone, copper, and galena, like the distinctive chert points found here, are not materials native to Mississippi: these high-prestige goods, like those found at the Pharr Mounds (see page 106), were acquired through long-distance trade networks.

Milepost 233.2 Witch Dance

✪ TRACE TOP 20, THE LIVING TRACE

This equestrian staging area is one of the more popular places to ride horses in all of Mississippi. The 18-mile Witch Dance Horse Trail is part of the Tombigbee National Forest; camping is reserved for cyclists, hikers, and equestrians. Amenities include restrooms, hitching posts, and plenty of picnic tables (at least one of which is accessible to those with disabilities) and grills.

Witch Dance boasts one of the most popular equestrian trails in Mississippi.

By their nature, legends grow tall out of a grain of truth. Legend has it that witches dance here, and that where they touch down the grass withers and dies. Be that as it may, and given that dead patches of grass are virtually ubiquitous, there is truth to the fact that plenty of souls succumbed to the Trace's hardships and "crossed over" while traveling it. But while the name is evocative, there's nothing witchy about the site itself.

Milepost 241.4 Chickasaw Agency
ARCHAEOLOGY AND AMERICAN INDIANS

This is just an informational panel and parking lot marking the fact that from 1801 to 1825, this location served as headquarters for the federal government's Indian agent, a diplomat and mediator for the Chickasaw.

Milepost 243.1 Davis Lake
NATURAL WONDERS

This is the access point for a US Forest Service recreation area and campground. See page 146 in Appendix 2 for more information on this facility.

Milepost 243.3 Hernando de Soto
CIVIL WAR AND OTHER MILITARY HISTORY

Enjoy a picnic near where the legendary Spanish explorer of the Mississippi spent the winter of 1540–41. According to the Pontotoc Chamber of Commerce, it was at this camp on Christmas Day 1540 that the first European–Indian marriage in America was held between Juan Ortiz and Sa-Owana, a Seminole princess held captive by the Spaniards. The event is depicted in a mural in the Pontotoc post office.

Milepost 245.6 Monroe Mission Station
ARCHAEOLOGY AND AMERICAN INDIANS

Another spot to enjoy a picnic, this one is near the former site of an Indian mission and school founded by Presbyterians in 1822.

Milepost 249.6 Tockshish
KAINTUCK BOATMEN AND THE POSTAL ROAD

We're establishing a pattern: here's yet another place to enjoy a picnic, this time near the site of McIntoshville, where Mississippi's second post office was established in 1801 as a postal relay station between Nashville and Natchez.

Tockshish once had a mission school and church. Such schools proved to be excellent training grounds for young Chickasaw, who used the skills they learned here to assume leadership responsibilities after the tribe's subsequent removal to Oklahoma.

Beautiful blooms grace many stops along the Parkway.

Milepost 251.1 Chickasaw Council House
ARCHAEOLOGY AND AMERICAN INDIANS

In the 1820s the council house at Pontatok became the capital of the Chickasaw Nation. Here tribal leaders met to adopt laws, set policies, and sign treaties.

Milepost 251.9 Black Belt Overlook
NATURAL WONDERS

The overview here highlights an essential cornerstone of local culture for hundreds of years. *Black Belt* refers to a swath of earth that reaches eastward from Mississippi and across nearly all of Alabama—a region known for rich black soil that is ideal for growing crops, especially cotton. Limestone deposits that once lined an ancient seafloor transformed over millions of years into uncommonly fertile soil. At first a grassland prairie, then a cotton-rich region, the Black Belt still supports the local people as a superior pasture for livestock.

Tupelo

> *They die well who die for faith and home and native land.*
> —From the DAR marker near Tupelo that commemorates the Battle of Ackia

The modern city of Tupelo, with more than 38,000 citizens, stands upon ancient, hallowed ground. From the earliest Indian settlement, the Tupelo area was linked

Interactive exhibits and suggested itineraries for weekend getaways, historical tours, and Elvis Journeys are available at the **Tupelo Visitors Center** (399 E. Main St.; 662-841-6521, tupelo.net).

to the outside world via the Natchez Trace. When Spanish explorer Hernando de Soto passed through this area in 1540, he encountered an established Chickasaw civilization nestled in the wooded hills and valleys. The Chickasaw, who had a reputation as fierce fighters, ultimately drove de Soto westward toward the Mississippi River, the "discovery" of which he is perhaps most famous for.

In 1736, at the height of the French and Indian War, a bloody battle erupted near Tupelo between the Chickasaw, aided in part by the British, and the combined invading forces of the French and the Choctaw. Known as the Battle of Ackia, the engagement left the area in British control, and this in part contributed to the Crown's eventual domination of North America.

The Civil War also left its mark upon the Tupelo area. The Battle of Tupelo, in mid-1864, pitted Union troops against Confederate cavalry bent on controlling railroad traffic supplying the Union campaign against Atlanta.

Formally incorporated in 1870 and named after a native tree, Tupelo became an early rail hub with the convergence of the Mobile & Ohio, the Kansas City, and the Memphis & Birmingham lines here in 1887. In 1934, during the Great Depression, Tupelo became the first city in the US to receive affordable hydroelectric power through the Tennessee Valley Authority.

Tupelo has several notable attractions, not the least of which is the birthplace of **Elvis Presley,** which has greatly expanded its offerings in recent years (see next page). Another standout is **Tupelo Buffalo Park,** home to several exotic animal species and a bison herd that includes Tukota, a rare white buffalo who keeps the legendary mystical power of such animals alive. (Sioux Indians believe that a white buffalo is the most sacred of all living animals, and that to see one is a great blessing.) The buffalo is particularly germane to the Trace story, for this great animal helped in large part to carve the original trails.

Tupelo Buffalo Park and Zoo *2272 N. Coley Road, Tupelo; 662-844-8709, tupelobuffalopark.com. Open Monday–Thursday, 9 a.m.–4 p.m.; Friday and Saturday, 9 a.m.–5 p.m.; Sunday, 11 a.m.–4 p.m.; closed December 25. Admission: $11 for adults, $9 for seniors (65+), free for children younger than 1 year old. Pony rides, guided trail rides, and bison tours also available for a fee. From the Natchez Trace Parkway, exit at milepost 262.0 onto MS 178/McCullough Boulevard, heading west. In 2.6 miles turn left (south) onto Coley Road; the park is 0.7 mile ahead, on your left.*

Milepost 260.0 Elvis Presley's Birthplace and Boyhood Haunts
THE LIVING TRACE

Note: *Allow at least an hour for this side trip.*

> *When I was a child, ladies and gentlemen, I was a dreamer. I read comic books, and I was the hero of the comic book. I saw movies, and I was the hero in the movie. So every dream I ever dreamed has come true a hundred times.*
>
> —Elvis's acceptance speech for the 1970 Ten Outstanding Young Men of the Nation Award presented by the Jaycees

Whether or not you're an Elvis Presley fan, it's worthwhile to make a side trip off the Parkway to the birthplace of the "Southern version of the Horatio Alger hero" who has sold more records—over a billion globally—than any person on Earth. In a quiet Tupelo neighborhood, you can go inside the tiny two-room, shotgun-style house built by Elvis's father, Vernon. Here, Gladys Presley gave birth to Elvis Aaron and his stillborn twin, Jesse Garon. The modesty of the house—especially if you've ever been to Elvis's opulent Memphis mansion, Graceland—is deeply touching. It explains why Elvis, even when his wealth and fame had far exceeded his dreams, was also known for his generosity and his identification with working-class people.

Staffed by knowledgeable employees who are also Elvis devotees, the attraction includes an event center, an amphitheater, a lake with a fountain, a couple of statues, a picnic pavilion, a museum, a gift shop, and a chapel.

House of royalty: Elvis Presley, aka The King, was born in this humble shotgun abode.

A chapel on the grounds of the Elvis Presley Birthplace

Tupelo also offers a self-guided tour of some of the most significant Elvis-related sites, such as where he bought his first guitar (**Tupelo Hardware**) and where he hung out (**Johnnie's Drive-In**). The **Parkway Visitor Center** (milepost 266; 662-680-4027) has maps available.

Elvis Presley Birthplace *306 Elvis Presley Drive, Tupelo; 662-841-1245, elvispresleybirthplace.com. Open Monday–Saturday, 9 a.m.–5 p.m. (until 5:30 p.m. May 1–September 30); Sunday, 1–5 p.m.; closed Thanksgiving and December 25. Combined tours of the house, museum, and church are $18 for adults, $14 for seniors (60+), $8 for children 7–12, and free for children under 12. House-only tours are $8 for adults and seniors, $5 for children 7–12, and free for children under 12. Exit the Parkway at milepost 260.0 onto MS 6/Main Street in Tupelo, and follow it east through town about 4.5 miles, across railroad tracks. Just past Veterans Memorial Boulevard, take a left on Elvis Presley Drive and follow the signs.*

Milepost 260.0 Tupelo National Battlefield
CIVIL WAR AND OTHER MILITARY HISTORY

One mile east of the Parkway, you can visit this small street-corner park that commemorates the Civil War Battle of Tupelo (also known as the Battle of Harrisburg), which took place July 14–15, 1864. The site, just past Monument Drive on the right at 2005 Main St., has no parking, however, so you'll have to park on the street or in a nearby lot. You'll see a monument to Confederate troops dating back about a hundred years; a monument to the losses on both sides is more recent. Confederate losses included 210 killed, 1,116 wounded, and 47 missing; Union losses amounted to 77 killed, 559 wounded, and 38 missing.

Milepost 261.8 Chickasaw Village Site
ARCHAEOLOGY AND AMERICAN INDIANS

You'll find signs with interpretive audio in the exhibit shelter, all vetted by the Chickasaw Nation. Concrete curbs on the ground mark the outline of Chickasaw seasonal dwellings and a fort. Exhibits describe daily life and early history.

A 0.5-mile, 20-minute out-and-back on a level, self-guided interpretive trail features plants used by the Chickasaw. Back on the Parkway, you can continue north for 2 miles alongside the road on a trail to the Old Town Overlook (see below); this is the Blackland Prairie Trail, a segment of the Natchez Trace National Scenic Trail (see page 51). From the Old Town Overlook, you can continue north another 2 miles to reach the **Parkway Visitor Center** (see below).

This pond near Old Town Overlook makes for a nice picnic spot just off the Parkway.

Milepost 263.9 Old Town Overlook
ARCHAEOLOGY AND AMERICAN INDIANS

This area was once the heart of Chickasaw territory. (*Old Town* refers to a Chickasaw village that once stood near Old Town Creek.) From here you can hike 2 miles south along the Blackland Prairie Trail to the Chickasaw Village Site (see previous page), or you can hike 2 miles in the other direction to the **Parkway Visitor Center** (see next milepost).

Milepost 266.0 Parkway Visitor Center and Headquarters

✪ TRACE TOP 20, NATURAL WONDERS, NPS INFORMATION

This can't-miss stop, right on the Parkway, is the only Trace information center open year-round. The staff here can answer your questions and point out ways to make your trip even more enjoyable. You'll find interactive exhibits covering various aspects of Trace life, a free introductory film, brochures on area attractions, and a shop with Trace-related books and gifts. For more mental refreshment, you can

A nature trail at the Parkway Visitor Center is a great place for you and your pet to stretch your legs.

stroll on the paved, self-guided **Beech Spring Trail,** which takes you about 15–20 minutes through an area of forest regrowth. The visitor center is also the northern trailhead of the **Blackland Prairie Trail,** part of the Natchez Trace National Scenic Trail (see page 51). To the left of the headquarters as you're facing it is a quick access road into Tupelo, along which you'll find many motels, retail outlets, and restaurants. Finally, note that the visitor center has one of just five bike-only campgrounds along the Parkway (see page 148).

Parkway Visitor Center *2680 Natchez Trace Parkway (milepost 266.0); 662-680-4027, nps.gov/natr. Open daily, 9 a.m.–4:30 p.m., except Thanksgiving, December 25, and January 1.*

Milepost 266.0 Brices Cross Roads National Battlefield Site
CIVIL WAR AND OTHER MILITARY HISTORY

Note: Allow about 2.5 hours for this side trip.

The Battle of Brices Cross Roads has been studied at many war colleges because of Confederate Major General Nathan Bedford Forrest's ability to overcome substantial odds. Shelby Foote wrote in *The Civil War: A Narrative, Red River to Appomattox,* "The enemy had a close to two-to-one advantage in men, as well as nearly three times as many guns, but Forrest believed that boldness and the nature of the terrain, which he knew well, would make up for the numerical odds he faced."

Forrest was a threat to Union General William Tecumseh Sherman's supply line, which was vital to his mission to capture the key city of Atlanta. Sherman ordered Union forces at Memphis, Tennessee, to march south into Mississippi to find and, ideally, wipe out Forrest and his cavalry.

On the morning of June 10, 1864, Confederate troops engaged Union forces near Baldwyn, Mississippi, along the narrow wooded lanes around Brices Cross Roads. Forrest, who had a near-prescient grasp of what the Union commander Brigadier General Samuel D. Sturgis would do, mounted a bloody daylong battle against a much larger Union army. A long-lasting rain that resulted in wagon-hub-deep mud was followed by high heat—both factors that Forrest also used in his rout, considered one of the most decisive victories of the American Civil War.

Ultimately, Forrest acquired a large number of arms and ammunition and 1,600 captured men who were on retreat. Counting the captured men, Union troops suffered five times the losses of the Confederates. Yet for the sureness of the victory, Sherman's tactic of engagement had successfully kept Forrest away from Union supply lines—and so his March to the Sea continued.

Total Confederate losses: 96 killed, 386 wounded, and 492 missing; total Union losses: 223 killed, 394 wounded, and 1,623 missing.

Brices Cross Roads National Battlefield Site *MS 370, Guntown, about 10 miles north of Tupelo; 800-305-7417, nps.gov/brcr. From the Parkway exit at milepost 266.0 in Tupelo, head north on MS 145 and, in about 3.3 miles, turn left across the road to access the entrance ramp for US 45 North. In about 9.6 miles, exit at MS 370/Bethany Road. To go to the battlefield (open daily, sunrise–sunset), turn left onto MS 370 and drive about 3.7 miles to the first interpretive stop, on the left.* **GPS: N34° 30.479' W88° 43.404'**

Or turn right onto MS 370 at the intersection and then take the first right onto Grisham Street for **Mississippi's Last Stands Visitor and Interpretive Center** *(607 Grisham St., Baldwyn; 662-365-3969, finalstands.com). The center offers exhibits and an audiovisual presentation; we recommend stopping here before you go to the battlefield. Open Tuesday–Saturday, 9 a.m.–5 p.m.; admission is $5 for adults and $2 children under age 12.*

Between Tupelo and the Mississippi–Alabama State Line

Milepost 269.4 Confederate Gravesites

CIVIL WAR AND OTHER MILITARY HISTORY, THE OLD TRACE

A 5-minute walk on the Old Trace takes you to the graves of 13 unknown Confederate soldiers, whose faintly etched tombstones line the old roadway that once was a prominent final resting place along a busy route. It is unknown whether these men perished from wounds or disease, but their graves speak clearly of a chapter in Trace history buried here in the Mississippi soil.

Milepost 275.2 Dogwood Valley
NATURAL WONDERS, THE OLD TRACE

Stretch your legs for 15 minutes or so as you walk through a large stand of exception-ally mature dogwood trees, some more than 100 years old. The up-and-down loop trail of about 2.5 miles offers beauty whether the dogwoods are in bloom or not.

Milepost 278.4 Twentymile Bottom Overlook
THE OLD TRACE

The overlook is at the end of a road branching off the Parkway with no easy turn-around, so RVs are not advised. The low area along the stream is typical of the landscape through which the Old Trace passed, providing a sharp contrast to the modern conveniences of today's Parkway.

Milepost 283.3 Donivan Slough
NATURAL WONDERS

You'll be welcomed by a single picnic table and, in season, wildflowers on this 15-minute flat, circular singletrack trail. It takes you through a dense forest where you can gain an understanding of how occasional flooding influences the variety of plants here. Along the way, a secluded bench lets you soak up all that the woods have to offer.

Milepost 286.3 Browns Bottom
NATURAL WONDERS

While no sign marks the stop at the time of this writing, it does have a parking area, a lone picnic table, and a small pond that allows fishing if you have a state license. **GPS: N34° 28.214' W88° 25.548'.**

Milepost 286.7 Pharr Mounds
ARCHAEOLOGY AND AMERICAN INDIANS

Eight mounds rise from across a majestic field, but they're not particularly close and only a few are truly visible. It's tempting to enter the field and approach the earthworks, but to protect the mounds, please refrain. And note that these sites are still sacred to Indians whose ancestors lived here. This site was occupied during the Late Archaic era, but these burial mounds were built during the Middle Woodland period, between AD 1 and 200.

Ranging from 2 to 18 feet tall, the mounds are distributed over about 90 acres and comprise one of the largest Middle Woodland ceremonial sites in the south-eastern United States. The National Park Service excavated four of the mounds in

1966. Inside the mounds are fire pits and low, clay platforms. Cremated and unburned human remains were found in and near these features, as were ceremonial artifacts including copper spools and other copper objects, decorated ceramic vessels, lumps of galena (shiny lead ore), a sheet of mica, and a greenstone platform pipe. The copper, galena, mica, and greenstone did not originate in Mississippi; rather, they were brought here over long distances through extensive trade networks. Such ritually significant nonlocal items typify the Middle Woodland period.

Milepost 293.2
Tennessee–Tombigbee Waterway and Jamie L. Whitten Bridge
THE LIVING TRACE

In 1946 the US Congress authorized the US Army Corps of Engineers to plan for a canal between the Tennessee and the Tombigbee Rivers, which would cut the distance between the developing industrial regions of the mid-South and the ocean ports on the Gulf of Mexico by more than 800 miles. The connection created 459 navigable water miles between the Gulf of Mexico and the Tennessee River.

The Tenn–Tom, as the waterway is nicknamed, forms a 234-mile-long, 300-foot-wide by 9-foot-deep transportation artery connecting west-central Alabama with northeastern Mississippi. In May 1971 President Richard Nixon turned the first spade of earth, and the Tenn–Tom opened for commercial traffic in January 1985. The most common commodities shipped by barge are forest products, petroleum by-products, crushed rock, and grains.

The Natchez Trace Parkway crosses the Tennessee–Tombigbee Waterway, a 234-mile man-made canal that connects the Tennessee River to the junction of the Black Warrior–Tombigbee River system.

The bridge and dam over the Tenn–Tom in this section is named for US Representative Jamie Lloyd Whitten (1910–1995). As a school principal, he was elected to the Mississippi House of Representatives in 1931. In 1941 he won a special election to fill a Congressional vacancy, and he served for 54 years, until his death—making him the longest-serving member of Congress from Mississippi.

The Tenn–Tom has seven campgrounds ($14–$24 per night) near but not directly adjacent to the Parkway (see our listing for **Piney Grove Campground** on page 146 in Appendix 2). Each provides water and electrical hookups, dump stations, wheelchair-accessible sites and facilities, playgrounds, and multiuse sports areas. Some campgrounds have fish-cleaning stations and sewer hookups; each site has an impact pad, grill, fire ring, picnic table, and lantern post. For reservations, call 877-444-6777 or go to recreation.gov/camping/gateways/441. Reservable sites are available March 1–October 31; first-come, first-served sites are available year-round.

Milepost 293.4 Bay Springs Lake
KAINTUCK BOATMEN AND THE POSTAL ROAD

This is the boat access for Bay Springs Lake and Dam, part of the Tennessee–Tombigbee Waterway (see previous milepost).

Milepost 304.5 Tishomingo State Park
ARCHAEOLOGY AND AMERICAN INDIANS, NATURAL WONDERS

Less than 5 minutes off the Parkway, this beautiful state park is a great place for a lakeside picnic or overnight camping trip. Entrance fees are $4 per vehicle, plus 50¢ per person over six passengers. See page 43 in Chapter 2, "The Nuts and Bolts of Traveling the Trace," for more information about camping here.

Milepost 308.4 Cave Spring
ARCHAEOLOGY AND AMERICAN INDIANS

The Paleozoic hunters who used the Bear Creek Mound site (see next entry) probably used this water source. A short, easy, paved trail takes you to the cave's mouth. *Note:* Entering the cave is prohibited

Milepost 308.8 Bear Creek Mound
✪ TRACE TOP 20, ARCHAEOLOGY AND AMERICAN INDIANS

Standing on this exact spot, you are connected to nearly 10,000 years of human history. But aside from the anthropological interest, this is simply a great place to stretch your legs and roam around, making it nice for kids and dogs. Nearby is Bear Creek, which is accessible by foot.

The oldest prehistoric site on the Trace, Bear Creek Mound was first used by migratory hunters as a way station as early as AD 7000, or roughly 9,000 years ago. It was intermittently occupied thereafter for about 8,000 years, or until around AD 1300. Over those millennia, the people who inhabited this site evolved from primitive hunters to efficient hunters and gatherers and finally to an agriculturally based society.

The earthwork here was built in stages between AD 1200 and 1400, during the Mississippian period, for ceremonial or elite residential use. Burned daub, or mud plaster, found on the mound during archaeological excavation indicates the possible presence of a temple or a chief's residence. The site of a small residential village is nearby.

When the mound was first acquired by the NPS, its height had been worn down to about 4 feet due to farmers plowing and planting crops on it. Following its excavation in 1965, the mound was restored to its original estimated dimensions of about 8 feet high by 85 feet across the base.

MILEPOST 308.9 MISSISSIPPI-ALABAMA STATE LINE

ALABAMA (Mileposts 313.0–341.8)

Milepost 313.0 Bear Creek 🏕
NATURAL WONDERS

A lovely park graces the gentle, low bluffs of Bear Creek in this picnic area. With a picturesque view and creek access, this open yet secluded site is a perfect spot to watch children explore.

Milepost 317.0 Freedom Hills Overlook
NATURAL WONDERS

A paved trail that takes 10 minutes to walk at a moderate pace heads up to Alabama's highest point on the Parkway: 800 feet above sea level. Although the ascent is steep, especially at first, two benches provide rest stops along the way. The path is a delight in springtime when it's laced with dogwoods. The view at the top rewards you with a broad vista of green valleys and hills. Because

Pretty Bear Creek is a great place for family fun.
Photo: F. Lynne Bachleda

the elevation grade along the Trace is generally subtle and most settings look onto fields and forests, this vantage point's higher altitude provides a rare sense of overview.

Milepost 320.0 Shiloh National Military Park
CIVIL WAR AND OTHER MILITARY HISTORY

> *Note: This side trip is in Tennessee, but we've listed it here because of its proximity to the Alabama segment of the Parkway.*

Shiloh's tragic stillness makes it unique among Southern Civil War battlegrounds. One of its more poignant settings is Bloody Pond, where fallen soldiers—Union and Confederate alike—came to cleanse their wounds or quench their thirst. Its waters turned blood-red from all of the dead and dying soldiers who littered its banks.

Shiloh National Military Park was established in 1894 to preserve this scene of the first major battle, also known as Pittsburg Landing, in the Western Theater of the Civil War. The two-day battle, April 6–7, 1862, involved about 65,000 Union and 44,000 Confederate troops; nearly 24,000 soldiers on both sides were killed, wounded, or listed as missing. Shiloh proved a decisive victory for the Union, which forged on and seized control of the Confederate railway system at Corinth, Mississippi.

The battlefield covers about 4,000 acres. Also within the park's boundaries is **Shiloh National Cemetery,** along with several well-preserved prehistoric Indian mounds.

Shiloh National Military Park *1055 Pittsburg Landing Road, Shiloh, Tennessee; 731-689-5696, nps.gov/shil. Open daily year-round, 8 a.m.–5 p.m.; free admission. To get here from the Parkway exit at milepost 320.0 near Cherokee, Alabama, take US 72 West about 11.5 miles to Iuka, Mississippi. Exit right (north) onto MS 25, and in 15.2 miles cross into Tennessee—at the state line, MS 25 becomes TN 57. In 2.1 miles bear left at the fork onto Red Sulphur Road; in another 2.8 miles, turn left (west) onto TN 57. In 3.5 miles turn right (north) onto TN 142, which becomes TN 22. After 8.8 miles turn right onto Pittsburg Landing Road, and follow it 1.1 miles through the park until it dead-ends at the visitor center.*

Milepost 320.3 Buzzard Roost Spring 🚶
ARCHAEOLOGY AND AMERICAN INDIANS, NATURAL WONDERS

From a secluded parking lot, a short trail leads to Buzzard Roost Spring, where it's easy to picture how precious the small water source was to Trace travelers. A short descent on steep steps and then a steep gravel path reveals a quiet haven set in a cool and shady glen—the perfect retreat for a hot summer day. A shelter with exhibits tells the story of Chickasaw leader Levi Colbert, who owned a nearby stand to shelter travelers.

Levi was one of six sons of James Logan Colbert, a Scot who immigrated in 1736 and married into the Chickasaw tribe three times. Levi's brother, George, also a leader of the Chickasaw, ran a stand of his own; together they operated a ferry service across the Tennessee River (see Colbert Ferry, below).

The Chickasaw elevated Levi to a leadership position after he marshaled the boys and old men of the tribe to ambush an invading party of Muscogee.

In addition to the stand and ferry, Levi Colbert's holdings included a gristmill, salt springs, and a plantation powered by slave labor. He had a reputation for intelligence, hospitality, and prosperity. Some of his wealth came from compensation he received from the US government during negotiations with the Chickasaw.

Take a break at cool, shady Buzzard Roost Spring.
Photo: F. Lynne Bachleda

The Colbert brothers left their mark on both northwest Alabama and northeast Mississippi. This Parkway stop is in Colbert County, Alabama; Itawamba County, Mississippi, southwest of Colbert County just across the state line, is named for Levi Colbert, whose Chickasaw title was *Itawamba Minko* ("Bench Leader").

Milepost 327.3 Colbert Ferry
☺ TRACE TOP 20, KAINTUCK BOATMEN AND THE POSTAL ROAD

The main attraction here is the Tennessee River, as the 19th-century site of George and Levi Colbert's ferry is now submerged. Amenities include restrooms, fishing, a boat launch, and a bike-only campground (see page 148). Don't miss the expansive picnic area along the river, reached by taking the road that circles down, around, and behind the ranger station (closed at the time of this writing). This open space is a great place to take the kids and spend the day. If you have a boat, it's a great place to launch and enjoy time on the river; if not, you can still splash around in the water, have a picnic, or just toss a ball or Frisbee around.

Now Muscle Shoals has got the Swampers
And they've been known to pick a song or two (yes they do)
Lord they get me off so much
They pick me up when I'm feeling blue, now how 'bout you?

—"Sweet Home Alabama" by Lynyrd Skynyrd, 1974

A handful of exits on the Parkway in Colbert and Lauderdale Counties in Alabama lead you to what is now commonly known as The Shoals. Once known as the Tri-Cities, **Florence, Sheffield,** and **Tuscumbia** eventually added their newer neighbor, **Muscle Shoals,** and became the Quad Cities. But with the 2013 documentary *Muscle Shoals* and more recognition for the area coming from music tourism, the whole region has started taking advantage of Muscle Shoals' newfound fame.

Speaking of which, the main entity that kicked off the Shoals as a hotbed of music was **FAME Recording Studios** (256-381-0801, famestudios.com). Launched mainly as a music-publishing outfit in downtown Florence by Rick Hall, Billy Sherrill, and Tom Stafford, its name is an acronym for "Florence Alabama Music Enterprises." But soon Hall became the sole owner, moved the operation across the Tennessee River to Muscle Shoals, and began to ramp up the recording part of the business.

Muscle Shoals Sound Studio is once again a working recording facility.

In 1961 the first hit record became Arthur Alexander's "You Better Move On." The business moved again in 1963 to its current location at 603 E. Avalon Ave. in Muscle Shoals, and the hits piled up from artists such as Aretha Franklin, Etta James, Wilson Pickett, Bobbie Gentry, Clarence Carter, Candi Staton, and many more.

FAME's house band, The Muscle Shoals Rhythm Section—Barry Beckett, Roger Hawkins, David Hood, and Jimmy Johnson—broke away in 1969 to start **Muscle Shoals Sound Studio** (256-978-5151, muscleshoalssoundstudio.com), which is actually in Sheffield. Its address quickly became iconic after it was used as the name of Cher's 1969 album *3614 Jackson Highway*. Beckett, Hawkins, Johnson, and Hood became known as The Swampers after Lynyrd Skynyrd called them that in the final verse of "Sweet Home Alabama." After a few years, Muscle Shoals Sound Studio outgrew its building—originally a casket showroom—and moved to 1000 Alabama Ave., on the banks of the Tennessee River in Sheffield.

A tour bus for the band Alabama is part of the collections of the Alabama Music Hall of Fame.

The music industry—like the Singing River, as the Tennessee is known—has had its ebbs and flows and is very different from what it was in the 1960s and '70s, but music continues to play a major role in the area. FAME is still an active studio. The old Muscle Shoals Sound building has been restored and is once again a working studio, but much of its business comes from tours. The studio by the river, now known as **Cypress Moon** (256-335-6961, tinyurl.com/cypressmoon), houses a number of recording and production facilities. **Wishbone** in Muscle Shoals (256-443-9482, wishbonestudios.com) and **The NuttHouse** in Sheffield (256-381-0454, thenutthouse.com) are two heavily used local studios. All of these studios are located in Colbert County, which is also home to the **Alabama Music Hall of Fame** in Tuscumbia (617 US 72 W.; 256-381-4417, alamhof.org).

Across the river in Florence, upstart record label **Single Lock Records** (single lock.com) has established itself in the music industry, representing artists such as its cofounder John Paul White, along with an array of up-and-coming acts.

Colbert County Tourism provides group music tours ($40 per person; 256-383-0783, colbertcountytourism.org), and **Florence/Lauderdale Tourism** offers Swampette Tours led by David Hood's wife, Judy ($40 per person; 256-740-4141, visitflorenceal.com).

The NPS map recommends 20 minutes for the Rock Spring nature walk. Usually the Park Service's estimates are generous by 5–10 minutes, but Rock Spring has such a lovely, secluded variety of environments that you may want to linger much longer.

Milepost 330.2 Rock Spring
NATURAL WONDERS

Not to be confused with the Rocky Springs stop way back at milepost 54.8 in Mississippi (see page 84), Rock Spring has a self-guided trail along Colbert Creek—if you love water or you want a truly refreshing break, don't miss this stop. It has the quality of an enchanted forest, with changing scenery at every turn, and it provides useful information on trail markers about the surrounding animal and plant life. Be aware, however, that this area floods easily after heavy rains.

An easy singletrack loop trail with a rise at the back invites you to begin the hike, fording the spring-fed stream by treading on large chunks of dressed stone. These stones also make a great spot to sit in the sun and feel its warmth as you refresh your feet in the creek.

The trail meanders along the streambed, and within 5 minutes a bench under a shade tree invites you to sit and enjoy the surroundings. With a mix of hardwoods behind you and open wetland in front of you, you might see beavers (and their dams) or herons, if you're lucky.

The trail returns to the shady source of the spring, which flows from beneath a small overhang. The large rock at this site no doubt gave the place its name, and it's another good place to rest or even picnic (if you want to feast closer to your vehicle, there's a table at the trailhead). Many stops on the Trace don't fully remove you from the busyness of the blacktop, but Rock Spring's plush privacy takes you a world away.

Timber, the authors' dog, enjoys the creekside view at Rock Spring.

TENNESSEE (Mileposts 343.5–444)

Milepost 343.5 Cypress Creek
NATURAL WONDERS

An expansive, shady picnic area with easy access to the broad, sun-dappled creek where rock hounds can enjoy a quiet break and children can splash in the stream, which is easily accessible.

Milepost 346.2 Holly
NATURAL WONDERS

An open field removed from the Parkway offers high shade, several picnic tables, and easy access to the creek.

Milepost 350.5 The Sunken Trace
THE OLD TRACE

The original Trace was always a work in progress: it wasn't always a single path, nor was it always clear which way to proceed. The three sections of the original road here show how the route was relocated to avoid mud holes. The paths, not partic-ularly sunken, converge about 40 yards to the right of the paved parking area. They contrast the rough terrain the Trace's foot-weary had to trek with the Parkway's smooth surface.

Milepost 352.9 McGlamery Stand
KAINTUCK BOATMEN AND THE POSTAL ROAD

While this circle cul-de-sac doesn't have much of interest, a church and cemetery lie just beyond the Parkway boundary. The nearby village still bears the name of the stand that was founded here by a man named John McGlamery in 1849, nearly 40 years after Trace travel peaked in the 1810s. The stand was in business for about 12 years but closed at the advent of the Civil War in 1861.

Milepost 363.0 Sweetwater Branch
NATURAL WONDERS

An initial steep descent becomes a gently rolling out-and-back trail along Sweet-water Branch. One bench along the way and one at trail's end provide chances to soak in the water and enjoy the flora and bird presence here. Several easy access points permit wading in the tumbled-rock creek bottom. The final bench can be a good destination for a shady picnic. The round-trip should take about 30 minutes if you don't linger—but you'll probably want to, especially if there are wildflowers in bloom.

Interesting rock formations and a pretty creek make Glenrock Branch a top stop.

Milepost 364.5 Glenrock Branch

✪ TRACE TOP 20, NATURAL WONDERS

Set below the Parkway, this pull-off is a natural shady haven for family picnics. Adults can keep an eye on the kids while they explore this dappled glen set alongside the curve of a creek framed by a high limestone-cutaway bluff. A 0.6-mile trail leads to Upper Glenrock, another good place to picnic. Restrooms near the parking area are easily accessible while the creek itself and surrounding rock formations make this a delightful stop or even an all-day destination.

Milepost 367.3 Dogwood Mud Hole

THE OLD TRACE

There isn't anything here aside from a marker that helps remind you of what the Trace was like in periods of heavy rain (an often-impassable mud hole lies nearly a mile to the south). This stop is directly across the Parkway from a section of Old Trace that would make for a nice walkabout if you've been in the car for a while.

Milepost 375.8 Old Trace Drive
THE OLD TRACE

Note: Not suitable for travel trailers.

This one-way, 2.5-mile road follows the original Trace route. Traveling about 20 miles per hour is suggested, especially to enjoy the three overlooks with pretty views of the countryside. The pace and isolation here can help your mind and body gear down to the rhythm of the old road. Given the light traffic here, hikers can enjoy an out-and-back walk or return to their cars via the Parkway for about 1 mile, for a total loop hike of 3.5–4 miles.

Take your time along this stretch of the Old Trace. Photo: F. Lynne Bachleda

Milepost 377.8 Jacks Branch
NATURAL WONDERS

Another cool, shady drop below the level of the Parkway, this picnic spot has steps down from the roadway and provides a mossy carpet in the spring. It does have restrooms, but it isn't as easily accessible, or as scenic, as Glenrock Branch (see previous page), roughly 12 miles south at milepost 364.5.

Jacks Branch affords plentiful opportunities for picnicking.

Milepost 381.8 Napier Mine
THE LIVING TRACE

An information shelter tells about this open pit that was worked in the 19th century to supply ore for the tools the settlers needed. Shellfish deposited here throughout this part of Tennessee more than 400 million years ago have transformed into limestone layers containing phosphate, an important fertilizer at least since the 1860s.

Metal Ford is the Trace's premier swimming hole. Photo: F. Lynne Bachleda

Milepost 382.8 Metal Ford
◉ TRACE TOP 20, KAINTUCK BOATMEN AND THE POSTAL ROAD, THE OLD TRACE

If you're looking for a good old-fashioned swimming hole, Metal Ford is your stop. With picnic tables and a grassy, open field, it gives you all the ingredients for a daylong summer adventure. Metal Ford takes its name from the metal-like, smooth-stoned Buffalo River bottom. With a gentle current that varies between ankle- and chest-deep, this is a nostalgic place to let your cares be washed downstream. In July swimmers enjoy inviting water temperatures and easy maneuvering on the rock bottom. A short trail to the right as you face the river will take you to an old millrace, a river channel whose current once fed Steele's Iron Works to produce primitive pig iron in the early 1800s. The now-dry channel looks like numerous segments of the Sunken Trace. John McLish operated a nearby stand during some of the Trace's prime years, between 1812 and 1822, capitalizing on this spot where Trace travelers forded the Buffalo River.

Milepost 385.9 Meriwether Lewis Visitor Information Center Site

◉ TRACE TOP 20, NPS INFORMATION

This stop is rich with possibilities. Within its 300 acres you can learn about the probable suicide of famed explorer Meriwether Lewis, hike part of the Old Trace, picnic in a secluded cul-de-sac, and explore the beauty of both the ridge and hollow along Little Swan Creek. It's also home to Pioneer Cemetery (about

The monument to Meriwether Lewis is a broken shaft that symbolizes his untimely death.

100 gravesites) and the Grinder House, a re-creation of the kind of structure in which Lewis met his demise.

The campground here is one of the three along the Parkway run by the NPS, including **Jeff Busby** (milepost 193.1, page 95) and **Rocky Springs** (milepost 54.8, page 84). Like the others, it charges no fees. For more information on camping here, see page 41 of Chapter 2, "The Nuts and Bolts of Traveling the Trace." Several miles of hiking trails, in addition to the Old Trace section, offer a close look at young oak–hickory woods laced with dogwoods.

The primary attraction here is the grave of Meriwether Lewis,. co-commander of the Lewis and Clark expedition, who was traveling from St. Louis to Washington, DC. It is suspected that he committed suicide on the night of October 10, 1809, at Grinder's Stand, the first inn north of the Chickasaw Nation operated by whites. (The *d* in *Grinder* was a longstanding misspelling that had become accepted.)

Priscilla Knight Griner, wife of innkeeper Robert Griner, reported that Lewis was restless throughout the evening, and when the two shots rang out she was afraid to leave her room. The next morning, October 11, Lewis—who had a history of depression—was found barely alive with wounds to his head and chest. He died that day, at age 35, and was buried along the Trace. In 1848 the State of Tennessee erected the monument you see today over his gravesite: a broken shaft symbolizing the untimely conclusion to his life.

Milepost 386.6 English Camp Branch
NATURAL WONDERS

Down a grassy slope, you can enjoy the picnic table situated right beside a gently flowing waterfall.

Tennessee, in exchange for a cancellation of a $12,000 debt. Despite the economic coercion that produced this cession, the Chickasaws reaffirmed their loyalty to the United States during the War of 1812 by providing fighting men for the American army in the campaign against the Creek Red Sticks. One year after the battle of New Orleans, General Jackson "rewarded" them for their assistance: in 1816, Jackson and his fellow commissioners saw to it that the Chickasaws lost tribal title to all land on the northeast side of the Tennessee River, including a large southwestern portion of Middle Tennessee. After the Treaty of 1816, the only land remaining to the Chickasaws within the Tennessee region was in West Tennessee. Two years later, this too would belong to the United States.

The Trace here was the boundary line of Chickasaw lands ceded to the United States in 1805 and 1816.

Milepost 400.2 Sheboss Place
KAINTUCK BOATMEN AND THE POSTAL ROAD, THE OLD TRACE

A stand serving travelers on the Trace once stood here. Stands on Chickasaw land were granted tribal permission to operate, and the proprietors often had a direct link to the Chickasaw. The (alleged) story of Sheboss Place is that a Chickasaw man who spoke very little English married a white woman, and together they operated this rest stop. When Trace travelers arrived and began to converse and ask questions, the Chickasaw man would point to his wife and say simply, "She boss."

Milepost 401.4 Tobacco Farm and Old Trace Drive
THE LIVING TRACE, THE OLD TRACE

The primary interpretive element here is an old tobacco barn that still has some leaves suspended from the rafters. Other exhibits explain tobacco growing. A one-way, 2-mile drive along the Old Trace begins here. At first fairly rough and rutted, the path finally becomes a version of old pavement as it slopes you gently down the ridge to join the Parkway. Suitable for cars with regular and high clearance, this section isn't for RVs or cars with very low ground clearance.

Trace Tip

Hikers will especially enjoy Old Trace Drive's basically flat, slightly downhill grade, which is made even more pleasant by the valley overview through the fairly mature forest.

Milepost 403.7 Old Trace Walk
THE OLD TRACE

This 2,000-foot section of the original Trace dead-ends into the woods. The trail begins with a very short paved section but quickly becomes less civilized: although the NPS keeps the trail cut, you may come upon it in somewhat rough condition, and while it's basically flat, it's not a good place to wear open-toed shoes. If the grass is high, be sure to brush your legs and feet frequently to rid yourself of possible chiggers. See Chapter 2, "The Nuts and Bolts of Traveling the Trace" (page 28), to learn more about the harmful or aggravating creatures that you might encounter along the Parkway.

Milepost 404.7 Jackson Falls
✪ **TRACE TOP 20, NATURAL WONDERS**

Although a visit to Jackson Falls requires a 900-foot descent and then a return ascent, visitors invariably say it's worth the effort. When you pull into the parking area, take the trail to the right—a 0.5-mile trail to Baker Bluff veers to the left. You can walk in the woods to Baker Bluff and then return by roadside, if you prefer.

The hike to Jackson Falls—10 minutes at the most—is paved, bridged, and stepped down to the falls themselves, which makes it fairly easy. Here you'll find a large, circular limestone gorge that flows even in August—usually a dry month in Tennessee. If the water is flowing well you may see people using it as a natural slide. This current feeds into the Duck River. At the bottom a bench welcomes you, as does a cooler atmosphere and many flat rocks for poking about.

> ### Trace Tip
>
> The Jackson Falls stop can last a half hour or all day long, depending on how much you want to explore (and get wet). Restrooms and a picnic table are at the top of the trail.

Jackson Falls flows abundantly even during typically dry times.

Milepost 405.1 Baker Bluff Overlook
NATURAL WONDERS

This stop can also be reached by a roughly 0.5-mile hike from Jackson Falls (see previous milepost). The singletrack trail is hilly and, as is the case on most wooded paths along the Parkway, you'll want to watch out for poison ivy. At the Baker Bluff Overlook, you gaze down upon a working family farm in a picturesque setting. Exhibits here draw your attention to how conservation practices work with the earth.

ANDREW JACKSON, MAN OF THE TRACE

For land, for love, and for war, Andrew Jackson traveled the Natchez Trace at least five times. Probably his first trip on the old trail was in 1790, when he purchased some land about 25 miles north of Natchez near Springfield Mansion, where he later married the love of his life, Rachel Donelson Robards. After escorting his wife-to-be to Natchez via flatboat, Jackson returned home via the Trace. After he and Rachel married in August 1791, they also returned home by way of the old road.

Jackson's military affiliation with the Trace began when as major general he commanded his Tennessee Volunteers to proceed south to prevent British occupation of West Florida in the War of 1812. After his troops were stalled in Natchez for a month, Jackson received a letter from the Secretary of War indicating that plans had changed and that Jackson was to disband his men (some of them sick) where they were and let them fend for themselves. Jackson resisted this order—he was determined to take his men home, where they could be compensated for their service and properly discharged. On this march Jackson earned the nickname "Old Hickory," for his toughness. In 1815 Jackson again marched home on the Trace after defeating the British army at the Battle of New Orleans.

American-born of Scots-Irish heritage, with flaming red hair and a notorious temper, Jackson was orphaned at age 14. He succeeded at law, in the military, in land speculation, in duels, and in politics. By almost every account, his dealings with American Indians—including the Seminole, Creek, Choctaw, Cherokee, and Chickasaw peoples—were by any standard coercive and cruel, yet he raised several orphaned Indian children at his home in Nashville, The Hermitage.

Jackson's greatest triumph—his important and controversial presidency—was marred by the death of his beloved wife three months before he took office in 1829. He is remembered as a dominant early-19th-century personality, spawning Jacksonian Democracy as well as the so-called Age of Jackson. He was, in sum, much like the Natchez Trace he knew: demanding, unforgiving, difficult.

Milepost 407.7 Gordon House Historic Site 🚶 🚻 🪑

⊕ TRACE TOP 20, KAINTUCK BOATMEN AND THE POSTAL ROAD, THE LIVING TRACE

Here's another wonderful spot for a picnic, with open space, a shelter with picnic tables, and restrooms. The Gordon spirit still lingers around this 1818 house, home of John, Dolly, and their children. The Gordon House and Mount Locust (milepost 15.5, page 78) are the only two surviving structures from the Old Trace's early-1800s era. The Gordons built this brick home, the remainder of a plantation that once encompassed more than 1,500 surrounding acres. After first living in Nashville, the couple moved here to run the Duck River ferry, established in 1801 by troops as part of the new federal road the Natchez Trace. This section of the Trace ran from the Tennessee Valley Divide (milepost 423.9, page 128) southward to Colbert Ferry (milepost 327.3, page 111) on the Tennessee River.

John Gordon, who fought in the Creek War under Andrew Jackson, suffered from deteriorating health, due in part to his past military exploits, and he lived in this new house less than a year before he died in 1819. Faced with declining ferry business due to dwindling traffic on the Trace,

The Gordon House, though picturesque, is not open to the public at the time of this writing.

Dolly Gordon managed the farm until she died in 1859. Although the home is closed to the public, the NPS acquired it in 1973, and it was listed on the National Register of Historic Places in 1974.

To begin a 1-mile walk, stroll down the bank toward Fattybread Creek. If the footbridge is out, make your own way across to the field on the other side, and rest on the bench for a spell. Continue up a hill on this section of the Old Trace, and follow it toward the Duck River. You'll reach a level spot by the water that was the waiting grounds for the ferry, long since swept away by the cold currents of winter storms, but in operation until the bridge was built in 1896. A narrow path can take you closer to the Duck.

Power lines detract a bit from an otherwise-stunning view at Water Valley Overlook.

Milepost 411.8 Water Valley Overlook

NATURAL WONDERS

A lone picnic table sits high atop a rolling hillside. Although the commanding view is marred somewhat by TVA power lines, this is still a very pleasant spot with an isolated yet open feeling.

Milepost 423.9 Tennessee Valley Divide

NATURAL WONDERS

From the parking lot you can catch a connector to the Highland Rim Trail section of the National Scenic Trail (see page 51), which runs through this area. When Tennessee joined the Union in 1796, this watershed was the boundary between the United States to the north and the Chickasaw Nation to the south. This physiographic feature is part of the Highland Rim, which surrounds the Middle Tennessee basin.

Milepost 425.4 Burns Branch

NATURAL WONDERS

This stop is part of the Garrison Creek horse path and has the necessary hitching posts to prove it; see Chapter 3, "The Many Ways to Travel the Trace" (page 46), for more information on horseback riding. Those not on horseback, however, will find it a memorable picnic spot, with four tables generously spaced alongside a placid, cooling creek. It's also a trailhead for the Highland Rim section of the National Scenic Trail (see page 51).

Milepost 426.3
War of 1812 Memorial and Old Trace

THE OLD TRACE

The US Army stationed at Garrison Creek cleared this section of the Trace in 1802–03 and continued clearing southward with the consent of the Chickasaw Nation. You can take an easy 2-mile hike to Garrison Creek under a mature forest canopy that can be glorious in the fall. You'll see a monument to the War of 1812 here.

Milepost 427.6 Garrison Creek

This monument honors War of 1812 soldiers buried along the Old Trace.

CIVIL WAR AND OTHER MILITARY HISTORY

Along with Witch Dance way back in Mississippi (see page 98), this is the main stop for equestrian enthusiasts on the Parkway. Named for a nearby 1802–03 US Army post, this area is a trailhead for horseback riders and hikers. It's a nice picnic spot along the waterway, with plenty of room for horse trailers to maneuver. A map sign shows the hiking and horse trail loop. See page 51 in Chapter 3, "The Many Ways to Travel the Trace," for more information on this trail.

Milepost 428.9 Leiper's Fork
THE LIVING TRACE

This quaint, quirky small town is just off the Parkway exit at TN 46. Leiper's Fork was established in 1785 as Bentontown, named after Thomas Hart Benton, who represented Missouri as a US Senator from 1821 to 1851. (His great-grandnephew, also named Thomas Hart Benton, was a 20th-century artist who, along with Grant Wood and John Steuart Curry, helped define the Regionalist style of painting.) You can see the location of the Benton home, but another house has since been built atop the Benton foundation.

The community's name was changed when the Bentons left for Missouri. Settlers from Hillsboro, North Carolina, changed the name to Hillsboro. Then, early in the 20th century, the name was changed to Leiper's Fork, after nearby Leiper's Creek.

Today Leiper's Fork works hard at keeping a true small-town feeling alive in its scenic community. Live music, good food, and outdoor movies on the lawn in summer are hallmarks. For a visitors' guide, go to visitleipersfork.com.

NORTHERN MAGNET: NASHVILLE'S SALT LICK

If you look at a modern-day map of Nashville, you can see that the old major artery roads resemble the spokes of a wheel that once came together at what is today's **Bicentennial Capitol Mall State Park,** a 19-acre urban green space just north of the State Capitol. Animals made these original roads. Fossils indicate that, starting 2.5 million years ago, Pleistocene mammals converged here, including giant camels, elephant-like mastodons, wild horses, deer, ox-size ground sloths, native pigs called peccaries, and saber-toothed tigers. More recently, powerful and plentiful herds of buffalo trod the same paths. They all came in search of a salty sulfur spring, to imbibe the remains of an ancient sea that covered West and Middle Tennessee beginning 570 million years ago.

At the Mall you can visit the site of this ancient spring, which is arguably what brought the Natchez Trace and its Parkway into existence. To find it, ask a ranger at the welcome center near the State Capitol end of the Mall, or on the Mall, face the Capitol on the hill. From the street below the Capitol, James Robertson Parkway, come down about a third of the length of the Mall, and then head left toward the Cumberland River along a winding concrete-paved path. A freshwater fountain marks the general spot of the spring—a powerful magnet that helped to create the Natchez Trace—but underneath the pavement the historic, salty sulfur blend still swirls beneath your feet on it way to the river.

In addition, the state park offers many outdoor historical and cultural exhibits on Tennessee. Fountains at the River Wall offer refreshment on hot days.

Bicentennial Capitol Mall State Park *At the foot of the Tennessee State Capitol, bounded by James Robertson Parkway, Jefferson Street, and Sixth and Seventh Avenues; 615-741-5280, tnstateparks.com/parks/info/bicentennial-mall. Open daily year-round, sunrise–sunset. The Visitor Center (600 James Robertson Parkway) is open Monday–Friday, 8 a.m.–4:30 p.m.*

Milepost 437.2 Timberland Park
○ **TRACE TOP 20, THE LIVING TRACE, NATURAL WONDERS**

This day-use park is operated by Williamson County Parks & Recreation but can be accessed directly from the Parkway. Amenities and attractions include a butterfly garden, interpretive center, and day camps. An ADA-accessible pathway makes this one of the best spots on the Parkway for people with disabilities. Open daily, 9 a.m.–6 p.m., free admission; 615-232-4154, tinyurl.com/timberlandpark.

The TN 96 double-arch bridge has been nationally honored for its innovative design.

Milepost 438.0 Birdsong Hollow
✪ TRACE TOP 20, THE LIVING TRACE

You have a few ways to enjoy this area. The view from the bridge at 155 feet above the valley floor, which you can access from the milepost pull-off on the north side of the span, is a very good one. It's essential, however, that you pull off the Parkway at the exit for TN 96 on the southern side of the bridge and drive down into Birdsong Hollow to appreciate the bridge's soaring, elegant construction. You can easily turn around and get right back on the Trace.

This is the nation's first arch bridge constructed with concrete segments, and it spans a hefty 1,648 feet. The bridge's arches are designed to support the deck without evenly spaced spandrel columns, resulting in an unencumbered appearance. In all, 196 girder segments and 122 arch segments were used to produce it, at a cost of $11.3 million—a reasonable price, we think, for such a stunningly successful solution. The bridge has been honored with numerous design awards, including the Presidential Award for Design Excellence from the National Endowment for the Arts in 1995.

Milepost 444.0 Northern Terminus Intersection with TN 100
Although the NPS has plans for a welcome center here, at present just another of the Parkway's key bridges transports you to and from the Natchez Trace's "ribbon of time." The Parkway exit feeds you to the right onto TN 100, toward Nashville;

you can also travel on the bridge to cross over TN 100 for a sweep left that will send you west toward Fairview, Tennessee. If you're entering the Parkway from Nashville, go under the bridge, bear to your right, open your eyes and mind, and let the Natchez Trace Parkway time capsule work its magic.

Nashville

The first settlers in what is now known as Nashville were Indians of the Mississippian culture, who lived in the area around AD 1000–1400. They raised corn, built great earthen mounds, painted beautiful pottery—and then they mysteriously disappeared. Other Indians, the Cherokee, Chickasaw, and Shawnee, followed and used the area as a hunting ground.

The first white men to come to the area were French fur traders who established a trading post around 1717. The first settlement, however, was not established until 1779. It was then, on the banks of the Cumberland near the center of present downtown Nashville, that a band of pioneers led by Englishman James Robertson cleared the land and built a log stockade. This was Fort Nashborough, named in honor of General Francis Nash, who won acclaim in the Revolutionary War. John Donelson and some 60 families followed in April 1780 to settle the new community, which was then part of North Carolina. In 1784 the community's name was changed from Nashborough to Nashville.

Tennessee became the 16th state in 1796, and Nashville was made its permanent capital in 1843. By 1860 Nashville was a prosperous city, soon to be devastated by the Civil War. Because of its strategic location on the river and the railroad, the city was occupied by Federal troops for three years. The Battle of Nashville, fought in December 1864, was the last major offensive launched by the Confederate Army in the Western Theater of the war.

In the decades following the war, Nashville once again experienced growth in population, business and industry, and education. Another area of growth, of course, was country music, which gives Nashville its nickname of Music City USA. In 1963 Nashville and Davidson County consolidated into a single metropolitan government, which now encompasses more than 700,000 people (1.9 million in the greater metro area) and 533 square miles.

Nashville has many splendid attractions. One that pertains obliquely to the Trace story is **The Hermitage,** the home of Andrew Jackson, who frequently traveled the old road and earned his nickname, "Old Hickory," on it. The house and grounds were restored to look as they did during Jackson's retirement years, 1837–1845. Here you can see how a former president lived and learn about the humble origins of this grand home.

The Hermitage *4580 Rachel's Lane, Nashville; 615-889-2941, thehermitage.com. March 15–October 15, open daily, 8:30 a.m.–6 p.m.; October 16–March 14, open daily, 9 a.m.–5 p.m.; closed Thanksgiving and December 25. Admission: $20 adults, $17 seniors (62+), $15 students (ages 13–18), $10 kids (ages 6–12), $10 veterans, and free for active military and children under age 5; $54 family rate for two adults and two children. Located 12 miles east of downtown Nashville, The Hermitage is accessible from Exit 221A (The Hermitage) off I-40 and Exit 92 (Old Hickory Boulevard South) off I-65.*

Andrew Jackson's tomb is a highlight of a visit to The Hermitage. Photo: Zack Frank/Shutterstock

Appendixes

APPENDIX 1: INFORMATION SOURCES

Books

Bicycling the Natchez Trace: A Guide to the Natchez Trace Parkway and Nearby Scenic Routes, by Glenn Wanner (Pennywell Press, 2005). The bible for cyclists on the Parkway.

The Devil's Backbone: The Story of the Natchez Trace, by Jonathan Daniels (Pelican Publishing Company, 1998). A thorough and elegantly written history, beginning with the Hernando de Soto period.

Images of America: Building the Natchez Trace Parkway, by the Natchez Trace Parkway Association (Arcadia Publishing, 2012). This pictorial review, featuring more than 200 vintage images, was published to commemorate the 75th anniversary of the Parkway.

The Natchez Trace: A Pictorial History, by James A. Crutchfield (Rutledge Hill Press, 2000). First published in 1985, this is a great armchair-history browse, with black-and-white images of Trace sites, vintage illustrations, and maps.

Natchez Trace Parkway Survey (US Department of the Interior, 1940). This government report, which prepared the way for the modern Parkway, is a surprisingly engaging read for anyone who is deeply interested in the Trace's development. A digitized version is available at tinyurl.com/natcheztracesurvey.

Not Without My Father: One Woman's 444-Mile Walk of the Natchez Trace, by Andra Watkins (Word Hermit Press, 2015). The author of several Natchez Trace–related titles, Watkins wrote this memoir about trekking the Trace at a rate of 15 miles a day, assisted by her elderly father. A video blog of her journey is also available at vimeo.com/andrawatkins.

The Outlaw Years: The History of the Land Pirates of the Natchez Trace, by Robert M. Coates (Pelican Publishing Company, 2002). First published in 1930, this is a delicious if somewhat old-fashioned biography of some of the Trace's more unscrupulous characters. A digitized version is available at tinyurl.com/theoutlawyears.

60 Hikes Within 60 Miles: Nashville, by Johnny Molloy (fourth edition; Menasha Ridge Press, 2016). This outdoor guidebook includes a handful of Parkway hikes in Tennessee.

Travel Guide to the Natchez Trace Parkway Between Natchez, Mississippi, and Nashville, Tennessee, by Ilene J. Cornwell (Southern Resources Unlimited, 1984). It's out of print, and much of it is very likely out of date, but if you can get your hands on a copy, it's a wonderful compendium chock-full of facts organized by milepost.

A Way Through the Wilderness: The Natchez Trace and the Civilization of the Old Southwest, by William C. Davis (HarperCollins, 1995). The most scholarly of these titles, it's nonetheless a fascinating read.

Wildflowers of the Natchez Trace, by Stephen L. Timme and Caleb C. K. Timme (University Press of Mississippi, 2000). This handsome book profiles and includes illustrations of 100 wildflower species that grow along the Parkway.

Pamphlets

"The Natchez Trace: Indian Trail to Parkway," by Dawson A. Phelps (*Tennessee Historical Quarterly,* vol. XXI, No. 3, September, 1962). Reprinted by NPS partner Eastern National (see below) in 1998 and 2003, this thoroughly researched historical overview was written by the premier Natchez Trace authority of his day. The original journal article is available free at the JSTOR digital library (jstor.org/stable/42621760; registration required).

"Natchez Trace Parkway Teacher's Information Guide" (National Park Service, 2012). Written for educators by NPS staff, this treasure trove of facts about various Trace topics can be downloaded at tinyurl.com/ntpteachersguide.

Contacts

NATIONAL PARK SERVICE

NATCHEZ TRACE PARKWAY 800-305-7417, 800-300-7275 (emergencies), nps.gov/natr. One-stop shopping for all of your information needs: trip planning, driving and hiking maps, park history, and more.

For information about the **Natchez Trace National Scenic Trail,** visit nps.gov/natt. **Mississippi River Facts** (nps.gov/miss/riverfacts.htm) contains at-a-glance information about America's longest river, and **Indian Mounds of Mississippi** (nps.gov/nr/travel /mounds/index.htm) is a great place to learn more about the region's ancient mound-building culture.

EASTERN NATIONAL 877-628-7275, eparks.com. This private nonprofit partner of the NPS provides high-quality educational products and services in America's national parks and other public trusts. Look for Eastern National stores at the Parkway Visitor Center and contact stations elsewhere along the Parkway.

GENERAL NATCHEZ TRACE INFORMATION

NATCHEZ TRACE TRAVEL natcheztracetravel.com. Comprehensive independent website with trip-planning advice, maps, recommended points of interest, information on food and gas along the Parkway, a calendar of festivals and events, a guide to traveling the Trace by bike or motorcycle, and a bed-and-breakfast directory and reservation service (800-377-2770 or 615-522-4865, natcheztracetravel.com/bedandbreakfasts).

SCENIC TRACE scenictrace.com. Another comprehensive site, this one is cosponsored by the state tourism agencies for Alabama, Mississippi, and Tennessee.

Information by State: Travel and Tourism, Chambers of Commerce, and Cultural/Educational Resources

ALABAMA

ALABAMA TOURISM DEPARTMENT 800-ALABAMA (252-2262), 334-242-4169, alabama.travel

> **Alabama State Parks** 800-ALAPARK (252-7275), alapark.com
>
> **Colbert County Tourism & Convention Bureau** 256-383-0783, colbertcountytourism.org
>
> **Florence/Lauderdale Tourism** 256-740-4141, visitflorenceal.com
>
> **Muscle Shoals National Heritage Area** 256-765-5028, msnha.una.edu

AMERICAN INDIAN NATIONS

NATCHEZ NATION 918-489-5244, natcheznation.com

> **Chickasaw Nation** 580-436-2603, chickasaw.net
>
> **Choctaw Nation** 800-522-6170, choctawnation.com
>
> **Eastern Band Natchez** 803-988-1074 (no website)
>
> **Edisto Natchez-Kusso Tribe of South Carolina** 843-871-2126, natchezkussotribeofscedisto.website
>
> **Mississippi Band of Choctaw Indians** 601-663-7532, www.choctaw.org

MISSISSIPPI

VISIT MISSISSIPPI 866-SEE-MISS (733-6477), visitmississippi.org

> **Bed & Breakfast Association of Mississippi** 601-956-0084, missbab.com
>
> **City of Fulton** 662-862-4929, fulton.itawambams.com
>
> **City of Madison** 601-856-7116, madisonthecity.com
>
> **Clinton Chamber of Commerce** 601-924-5912, clintonchamber.org
>
> **Corinth Area Convention and Visitors Bureau** 662-287-8300, corinth.net
>
> **Craftsmen's Guild of Mississippi** 601-856-7546, craftsmensguildofms.org
>
> **Discover Houston** 662-456-2321, houstonms.org
>
> **Greater Starkville Development Project** 800-649-8687, starkville.org
>
> **Kosciusko–Attala Partnership** 662-289-2981, kapartnership.org, kosytrace.com
>
> **The Main Street Chamber of Leake County** 601-267-9231, leakems.com

Mississippi Delta National Heritage Area 662-846-4312, msdeltaheritage.com

Mississippi Department of Wildlife, Fisheries, and Parks 800-GO-PARKS (467-2757), mdwfp.com/parks-destinations; camping reservations: mississippistateparks.reserveamerica.com

Mississippi Hills National Heritage Area 662-269-2580, mississippihills.org

Okolono Area Chamber of Commerce 662-447-5913, okolonams.org

Pontotoc County Chamber of Commerce 662-489-5042, pontotocchamber.com

Port Gibson–Claiborne County Chamber of Commerce 601-437-4351, portgibsonchamber.wixsite.com/portgibsonchamber

Rankin County Chamber of Commerce 601-825-2268, rankinchamber.com /attractions

Raymond Chamber of Commerce 601-906-3006, raymondchamber.org

Ridgeland Visitor Center 800-468-6078, visitridgeland.com

Tishomingo County Tourism Council 662-423-0051, tishomingofunhere.org

Tupelo Convention and Visitors Bureau 662.841.6521, tupelo.net

Vicksburg Convention and Visitors Bureau 800-221-3536, visitvicksburg.com

Visit Jackson 800-354-7695, visitjackson.com

Visit Natchez 800-647-6724, visitnatchez.org

TENNESSEE

TENNESSEE DEPARTMENT OF TOURIST DEVELOPMENT 615-741-2159, tnvacation.com

Hardin County Convention and Visitors Bureau 800-552-3866, tourhardincounty.org

Hohenwald–Lewis County Chamber of Commerce 931-796-4084, hohenwaldlewischamber.com

Lawrence County Chamber of Commerce 931-762-4911, lawcotn.com/tourism

Nashville Visitors and Convention Corporation 800-657-6910, visitmusiccity.com

Tennessee Civil War National Heritage Area 615-898-2947, tncivilwar.org

Tennessee State Parks 888-TN-PARKS (867-2757), tnstateparks.com; camping reservations: reserve.tnstateparks.com

Visit Columbia 931-560-1575, visitcolumbiatn.com

Wayne County Chamber of Commerce 931-722-3575, waynecountychamber.org

Williamson County Convention and Visitors Bureau 615-591-8514, visitfranklin.com

APPENDIX 2: ACCOMMODATIONS NEAR THE PARKWAY

These listings are arranged south–north along the Parkway in Mississippi and Tennessee. *Note:* Except for one campground, accommodations in Alabama are located a half hour or more from the Parkway, so we've elected not to include them here.

The public campgrounds listed comprise state, National Park Service (NPS), US Forest Service (USFS), and US Army Corps of Engineers (USACE) facilities; NPS campgrounds are free and available only on a first-come, first-served basis.

GPS coordinates are provided for all accommodations. Bicyclists should plan ahead to find out the safest and closest exits. Pet-friendly accommodations are noted.

For an in-depth discussion of camping along the Parkway, see page 39. For additional information about accommodations near the Parkway and surrounding areas, check the tourism and visitor-bureau websites in the previous section.

Mississippi Hotels

Natchez (Milepost 0.0)

Visit Natchez See visitnatchez.org/businesses/stay for a detailed list of hotels, motels, and B&Bs in the area.

Lorman (Milepost 30.0)

Canemount Plantation Inn 4003 Alcorn Road (MS 552), West Lorman; 601–940–7206, canemountplantation.com. Renovated 1829 carriage house with six B&B suites. *About 6.7 miles northwest of the Parkway exit onto MS 552 in Lorman.* **GPS: N31° 53.653' W91° 07.601'**

Rosswood Plantation 2513 Red Lick Road; 800–533–5889, rosswoodplantation.net. Located midway between Natchez and Vicksburg, this B&B in an 1857 plantation mansion received an AAA Three Diamond Award. *About 4.6 miles east of the Parkway exit onto MS 552 in Lorman.* **GPS: N31° 49.115' W91° 00.699'**

Port Gibson (Milepost 37.0)

Collina Plantation Inn 100 Greenwood St.; 601–940–4560, collinaplantationinn.com. This B&B—an 1830s planter's cottage built by a local judge—sits on 8.5 acres. *About 1.9 miles north of the Parkway exit onto US 61 in Port Gibson.* **GPS: N31° 57.285' W90° 59.437'**

Isabella Bed and Breakfast 1009 Church St.; 601–437–5097, isabellabedandbreakfast.com. This 1880s Queen Anne Victorian has period furnishings. All rooms were updated in 2019. *About 2 miles north of the Parkway exit onto US 61 in Port Gibson.* **GPS: N31° 57.403' W90° 58.936'**

Learned (Milepost 67.0)

Harmony Farm Bed and Breakfast 3407 Learned Road; 601–946–7482, harmonyfarmofms.com. Cozy (350-square-foot) farm cottage. Pet-friendly; horse boarding available.

About 9.7 miles east of the Parkway exit onto MS 27 in Utica.
GPS: N32° 10.604' W90° 32.216'

Raymond (Milepost 79.0)

Mamie's Cottage Bed and Breakfast 2809 Dupree Road; 601-955-5777, tinyurl.com
/mamiescottage. Located on the grounds of the 1878 Dupree House, this circa–1840s
plantation cottage has two guest suites, each with its own entrance. *Technically Mamie's
is just 0.3 mile south of the Parkway, but because there's no exit here, reaching it requires
a detour of about 4.8 miles south and west of the Parkway exit onto MS 467 in Raymond.*
GPS: N32° 15.450' W90° 30.277'

Clinton (Milepost 87.0)

Comfort Inn & Suites Clinton 5010 Hampstead Blvd.; 601-925-8250, tinyurl.com
/comfortinnclinton. Indoor pool; free breakfast and Wi-Fi. *About 2.2 miles east
of the Parkway exit onto I-20 East and about 0.5 mile north of I-20 Exit 36.*
GPS: 32° 19.735' W90° 19.423'

Days Inn by Wyndham Clinton 482 Springridge Road; 601-925-5065, tinyurl.com
/daysinnclinton. *About 2.1 miles east of the Parkway exit onto I-20 East and about 0.4 mile
north of I-20 Exit 36.* **GPS: 32° 19.731' W90° 19.4710'**

Jackson Area (Milepost 101.0)

Note: The following two hotels are adjacent to I-55 North and thus most convenient to the
Parkway. Check visitjackson.com/stay-here for information on other Jackson-area hotels.

Embassy Suites by Hilton Jackson/North Ridgeland 200 Township Place, Ridgeland;
601-607-7112, tinyurl.com/embassysuitesridgeland. All-suite hotel with 24-hour
convenience store and free breakfast. *Though technically 0.5 mile west of I-55, a lack of
close-in exits means a detour of about 5.6 miles south and then north of the Parkway exit onto
I-55 South.* **GPS: N32° 26.443' W90° 09.012'**

Hyatt Place Jackson/Ridgeland 1016 Highland Colony Parkway, Ridgeland; 601-
898-8815, jacksonridgeland.place.hyatt.com. Pet-friendly hotel with all-day dining,
pool, and free Wi-Fi. *Though technically 0.4 mile west of I-55, a lack of close-in exits
means a detour of about 5.5 miles south and then north of the Parkway exit onto I-55 South.*
GPS: N32° 26.227' W90° 08.689'

Kosciusko (Milepost 160.0)

Kosciusko–Attala Partnership Visit kapartnership.org for accommodations listings
in the area.

French Camp (Milepost 181.0)

French Camp Bed & Breakfast Inn 100 Robinson Drive; 662-547-6835, frenchcamp
historicvillage.com/bed-and-breakfast. Comprises a main building consisting of two
connected mid-19th-century log cabins; a modern cottage built from salvaged period
materials; a refurbished 1800s dogtrot home; and a modern carriage house. Pets welcome

in the cottages but not the main B&B building. *Just off MS 413, about 0.3 mile east of the Parkway.* **GPS: N33° 17.691' W89° 23.954'**

Houston (Milepost 230.0)

Bridges-Hall Manor Bed & Breakfast 435 N. Jackson St., Houston; 662–456–4071, bridges–hallmanor.com. This renovated 1884 Victorian has five guest suites upstairs. A full Southern–style breakfast is served in the dining room. *About 4.3 miles northwest of the Parkway exit onto MS 8 in Houston.* **GPS: N33° 53.986' W89° 00.049'**

Tupelo (Milepost 260.0)

Fairfield Inn & Suites Tupelo 3071 Tom Watson Drive; 662-680-6798, tinyurl.com /fairfieldinntupelo. Basic motel with free breakfast and Wi-Fi. *About 2.3 miles northwest of the Parkway exit onto I-22/US 78 East.* **GPS: N34° 18.807' W88° 41.858'**

Hampton Inn & Suites Tupelo/Barnes Crossing 1116 Carter Cove; 662-821-0317, tinyurl.com/hamptoninntupelo. Basic motel with free breakfast and Wi-Fi. *Requires a 5.6-mile detour off the Parkway: exit onto I-22/US 78 West; then head south on I-45 and north on MS 145.* **GPS: N34° 18.202' W88° 42.026'**

La Quinta Inn & Suites by Wyndham Tupelo 1013 N. Gloster St.; 662-847-8000, tinyurl.com/laquintatupelo. Basic motel with free breakfast and Wi-Fi. *About 1.4 miles east of the Parkway exit onto McCullough Boulevard/MS 178.* **GPS: N34° 16.624' W88° 42.986'**

Moon Lake Farm Bed & Breakfast 3130 Endville Road, Belden; 662-420-1423, moonlakefarm.com. Country–style retreat on 75 acres. *About 6.5 miles east of the Parkway exit onto McCullough Boulevard/MS 178.* **GPS: N34° 18.428' W88° 50.243'**

Tombigbee State Park Cabins & Cottages 264 Cabin Drive, Tupelo; 662-842-7669, tinyurl.com/tombigbeesplodging. Seven air-conditioned cabins and one ADA-accessible cottage with central heat and air; all have bed and bath linens, basic kitchen equipment, a fireplace, and either a screened-in porch or a patio. *The park entrance is about 9.1 miles east of the Parkway exit onto McCullough Boulevard/MS 178 or 9.5 miles east of the Parkway exit onto I-22/US 78.* **GPS: N34° 13.985' W88° 37.830'**

Wingate by Wyndham Tupelo 186 Stone Creek Blvd.; 662-680-8887, tinyurl.com /wingatetupelo. *About 3.3 miles east of the Parkway exit onto I-22/US 78 East.* **GPS: N34° 17.127' W88° 40.246'**

Belmont (Milepost 297.0)

Belmont Historic Hotel 121 Main St.; 662-454-7948, tinyurl.com/belmonthotelms. Built in 1924, this Georgian–style hotel has 15 guest suites. *About 6.7 miles south of the southbound Parkway exit onto MS 25, or about 7.2 miles south of the northbound Parkway exit onto MS 4. See tinyurl.com/belmonthotelbikeroutes for the owner's recommended bike routes from the north and south.* **GPS: N34° 30.593' W88° 12.500'**

Tishomingo (Milepost 304.0)

Bear Creek Saloon Guest House 1338 MS 30; 334-332-3474, airbnb.com/rooms /3464120. Has two guest suites, each with king and queen beds plus a kitchen. Food and grocery delivery available. *About 1.2 miles west of the Parkway exit onto MS 30.* **GPS: N34° 38.302' W88° 10.279'**

Tishomingo State Park Cabins & Cottages 105 CR 90; 662-438-6914, tinyurl.com /tishomingosplodging. Six cabins (one ADA-accessible) and one ADA-accessible cottage; all have central heat and air, basic kitchen equipment, a fireplace, and either a screened-in porch or a patio. *About 4.5 miles east of the Parkway exit onto MS 25 North; the cabin loop is just south of the Parkway along Bear Creek, off CR 90.* **GPS: N34° 36.245' W88° 10.598'**

Iuka (Milepost 320.0)

Victorian Inn 199 CR 180; 662-423-9221, victorianinn.info. Unremarkable, no-frills motel complex built around a Victorian-era central building. Pet-friendly. *About 16.5 miles north of the Parkway exit onto MS 30 in Tishomingo, Mississippi, or about 13 miles west of the Parkway exit onto US 72 West in Cherokee, Alabama.* **GPS: N34° 48.238' W88° 13.896'**

Tennessee Hotels

Lawrenceburg (Milepost 369.9)

David Crockett State Park Cabins 1400 W. Gaines St.; 931-762-9408, reserve.tnstate parks.com/david-crockett/cabins. Seven LEED-certified cabins (one is pet-friendly); each has two bedrooms, two baths, a full kitchen, a gas fireplace, and a covered patio. *Located 15 miles east of the Parkway exit onto US 64.* **GPS: N35° 14.566' W87° 21.257'**

Hohenwald (Milepost 385.9)

Meriwether's Retreat 17 E. Third Ave.; 931-230-3790, meriwethersretreat.com. Comprises the Voorhees House (adults only), a 1915 Craftsman bungalow, and Olga's House (guests ages 12 and older), a modern B&B built on the site of a lace factory. *About 6.5 miles west of the northbound Parkway exit onto TN 20 or 8.7 miles west of the southbound Parkway exit onto US 412.* **GPS: N35° 32.645' W87° 33.109'**

Collinwood (Milepost 355.0)

Collinwood 355 Motel 101 Third Ave. S.; 931-332-6166, tinyurl.com/collinwood355. Two-story motel with a ground-floor studio (pet-friendly) and a full apartment upstairs. Restaurants located within walking distance. *About 0.5 mile west of the Parkway exit onto East Broadway Street in Collinwood.* **GPS: N35° 10.437' W87° 44.275'**

Miss Monetta's Country Cottage 400 W. Tennessee St.; 931-724-9309, missmonettas .com. Home-style accommodations consisting of two cozy cottages a block apart. Restaurants located within walking distance. *About 0.7 mile west of the Parkway exit onto East Broadway Street in Collinwood.* **GPS: N35° 10.559' W87 44.729'**

Santa Fe (Milepost 416.0)

Creekview Farm Retreat Bed & Breakfast 5177 Leipers Creek Road; 931-446-7993, tinyurl.com/creekviewfarm. Three-bedroom guest house on a working farm. *About 3 miles south of the Parkway exit onto TN 7 East in Santa Fe.*
GPS: N35° 45.911' W87° 11.553'

Leiper's Fork (Milepost 428.0)

Big East Fork Lodging 5528 Big East Fork Road, Franklin; 615-266-3414, bigeastfork .com/lodging. Collection of 11 private homes; entire houses and individual rooms are available for rent. *Though the rental office is technically 0.9 mile west of the Parkway, reaching it by road requires a considerable detour off the nearest Parkway exit: 2.6 miles northwest on TN 96, 0.3 mile southwest on Old Harding Pike, and then 2.3 miles south on Big East Fork Road. GPS is sketchy here, so call the rental office for the exact location.*
GPS (approximate): N35° 58.379' W87° 00.834'

Jackson's Sweet Tea Cottage 3758 Robinson Road, Thompson Station; 615-604-9791, jacksonsweetteacottage.rentals. Two-bedroom cottage on a 50-acre farm. *About 5 miles east of the Parkway exit onto TN 46.* **GPS: N35° 50.233' W87° 01.637'**

Mississippi Campgrounds

Natchez (Milepost 0.0)

River View RV Park and Resort 100 River View Parkway (GPS: 800 Martin Luther King Ave.), Vidalia, LA; 318-336-1400, riverviewrvpark.com. Just across the Mississippi River from Natchez in Louisiana, this private campground has 135 sites with numerous pull-throughs and back-ins. Amenities include electrical, water, and sewer hookups;

Rock Spring (milepost 330.2, page 116) is an excellent spot for a quick hike.

a dump station; showers; and a pool. *Just off LA 131, 5.6 miles west of the Parkway exit onto US 61 in Natchez.* **GPS: N31° 33.357' W91° 26.101'**

Natchez (Milepost 8.1)

Natchez State Park Campground 230-B Wickliff Road; 601-442-2658, tinyurl.com /natchezsp. See page 41 for more information. *Just off US 61, 1 mile east of the Parkway and about 10 miles north of Natchez.* **GPS: N31° 35.852' W91° 12.981'**

Port Gibson (Milepost 37.5)

Grand Gulf Military Park Campground 12006 Grand Gulf Road; 601-437-5911, grandgulfpark.state.ms.us. Public campground with 42 sites (pull-throughs and back-ins). Amenities include electrical, water, and sewer hookups; a dump station; showers; and laundry facilities. *On Grand Gulf Road, 10 miles northwest of the Parkway exit onto US 61 in Port Gibson.* **GPS: N32° 01.804' W91° 03.216'**

Rocky Springs (Milepost 54.8)

Rocky Springs Campground (NPS) 800-305-7417, nps.gov/natr. See page 40 for more information. *On the west side of the Parkway, about 20 miles northeast of Port Gibson.* **GPS: N32° 05.294' W90° 47.931'**

Clinton (Milepost 87.0)

Springridge RV Park 499 Springridge Road; 601-924-0947, springridgemhp.com /rv-park. Private campground with 42 sites. Amenities include full hookups, laundry, and cable TV. *On Springridge Road, about 2 miles southeast of the Parkway exit onto I-20 East and 0.2 mile south of I-20 Exit 36.* **GPS: N32° 19.314' W90° 19.391'**

Jackson Area (Milepost 102.0)

Timberlake Campground 143 Timberlake Drive, Brandon; 877-388-2267 or 601-992-9100, therez.ms.gov/pages/timberlake.aspx. Private campground with 108 sites (back-ins only) overlooking Ross R. Barnett Reservoir. Amenities include full hookups and showers. *Off North Shore Parkway, about 7 miles southeast of the Parkway Information Cabin exit in Ridgeland (just east of US 51 and I-55).* **GPS: N32° 23.141' W90° 02.364'**

Eupora/Ackerman (Milepost 193.1)

Jeff Busby Campground (NPS) 800-305-7417, nps.gov/natr. See page 40 for more information. *On the east side of the Parkway, about 33 miles northeast of Kosciusko.* **GPS: N33° 25.068' W89° 16.078'**

Houston (Milepost 195.2)

Stinkin Jim's Horse Camp 811 CR 52; 662-542-4665 (no website at press time). Private campground with 88 sites. Amenities include electrical and water hookups, a dump station, a laundry, showers, and 80 horse stalls. *About 5.3 miles northwest of the Parkway exit onto MS 8 in Houston.* **GPS: N33° 54.336' W88° 57.114'**

New Houlka (Milepost 243.1)

Davis Lake Campground (USFS) CR 124; 662-285-3264 (reservations: 877-444-6777, recreation.gov/camping/campgrounds/232256). This campground, in Davis Lake Recreation Area, has 24 sites. Amenities include electrical and water hookups, a dump station, and showers. *About 4 miles west of the Parkway exit onto Davis Lake Road/CR 413, 5.7 miles east of New Houlka and 17 miles southwest of Tupelo.* **GPS: N34° 02.849' W88° 56.338'**

Tupelo (Milepost 251.6)

Natchez Trace RV Park 189 CR 506; 662-767-8609, natcheztracervpark.com. Private campground with 32 sites (pull-throughs and back-ins). Amenities include electrical, water, and sewer hookups; a dump station; a laundry; and a pool. *Located 0.1 mile east of the Parkway exit onto CR 506 in Shannon, about 6 miles southwest of Tupelo.* **GPS: N34° 08.745' W88° 49.151'**

Tupelo (Milepost 259.7)

Trace State Park Campground 2139 Faulkner Road, Belden; 662-489-2958, tinyurl.com/tracestatepark. See page 42 for more information. *About 9 miles northwest of the Parkway exit onto US 278/MS 6 in Tupelo.* **GPS: N34° 15.618' W88° 53.187'**

Tupelo (Milepost 263.6)

Tombigbee State Park Campground 264 Cabin Drive; 662-842-7669, tinyurl.com/tombigbeestatepark. See page 43 for more information. *About 9.1 miles east of the Parkway exit onto McCullough Boulevard/MS 178 or 9.5 miles east of the Parkway exit onto I-22/US 78.* **GPS: N34° 13.985' W88° 37.830'**

Tupelo (Milepost 264.0)

Elvis Presley Lake and Campground CR 995; 662-620-6314, tinyurl.com/elvispresleylake. State-run facility with 16 camping pads; tent camping available in designated areas. Amenities include electrical and water hookups and a dump station. *About 2.6 miles east of the Parkway exit onto I-22/US 78.* **GPS: N34° 18.259' W88° 38.859'**

Tupelo (Milepost 266.0)

Campground at Barnes Crossing 125 Campground Road; 662-844-6063, cgbarnescrossing.com. Private campground with 50 sites (pull-throughs and back-ins). The amenities include full hookups, showers, cable, Wi-Fi, and a laundry. *Located 0.5 mile south of the Parkway exit onto MS 145 (just past the Parkway Visitor Center northbound).* **GPS: N34° 19.378' W88° 42.302'**

New Site (Milepost 293.5)

Piney Grove Campground (USACE) CR 3550; 662-728-1134 (reservations: 877-444-6777, recreation.gov/camping/campgrounds/232673). Open March–November, this public campground has 141 sites (pull-throughs and back-ins). Amenities include electrical and water hookups, a dump station, and showers. *On Bay Springs Lake north of MS 4, about 10 miles from the Parkway exit onto MS 4 West.* **GPS: N34° 34.103' W88° 19.671'**

Tishomingo (Milepost 303.9)

Tishomingo State Park Campground 105 CR 90; 662-438-6914, tinyurl.com
/tishomingostatepark. See page 43 for more information. *About 2.3 miles east of the
Parkway exit onto MS 25 North; the campground is on Haynes Lake, off State Park Road/
CR 90.* **GPS: N34° 36.700' W88° 12.060'**

Alabama Campground

Cherokee (Milepost 320.0)

Rose Trail Park Campground 9395 Riverton Rose Trail; 256-360-2764, rosetrailpark.org.
This municipal campground has 71 sites (back-ins only) on the shore of Pickwick Lake,
an impoundment of the Tennessee River. Amenities include electrical and water hookups,
showers, a dump station, and a boat ramp. *On Pickwick Lake north of US 72, 13 miles from the
Parkway exit onto Lee Highway/US 72 West.* **GPS: N34° 51.304' W88° 05.109'**

Tennessee Campgrounds

Lawrenceburg (Milepost 369.9)

David Crockett State Park Campground 1400 W. Gaines St.; 931-762-9408, reserve
.tnstateparks.com/david-crockett. See page 44 for more information. *Located 15 miles
east of the Parkway exit onto US 64.* **GPS: N35° 14.566' W87° 21.257'**

Hohenwald (Milepost 380.0)

Thousand Trails Wilderness Preserve–Natchez Trace RV Campground 1363 Napier
Road; 931-796-3211 or 800-288-7245, tinyurl.com/natcheztracervcampground.
This huge private RV campground has more than 500 sites, including dedicated tent-
camping and cabin areas. Amenities include electrical, water, and sewer hookups;
a dump station; showers; a laundry; a camp store; walking trails; a boat ramp; a play-
ground; and minigolf. *Located just east of the Parkway on Napier Road/TN 241, off the
Rack Clayton Road exit. RVs taller than 13.6 feet must exit the Parkway farther south, at
US 64, and take a 15-mile detour east on US 64, northeast on TN 240, and then northwest
on TN 241.* **GPS: N35° 26.061' W87° 28.420'**

Hohenwald (Milepost 385.9)

Meriwether Lewis Campground (NPS) 191 Meriwether Lewis Park Road; 800-305-
7417, nps.gov/natr. See page 41 for more information. *On the west side of the Parkway
inside Meriwether Lewis Park and National Monument, about 80 miles southwest of Nashville.*
GPS: N35° 31.344' W87° 27.332'

Hohenwald (Milepost 391.0)

Fall Hollow Campground and Bed & Breakfast 1329 Columbia Highway; 931-796-
1480; fallhollow.com. Private campground with 37 RV sites (3 pull-throughs available)
plus a tent area, a cabin, and a building housing a restaurant and B&B rooms. Other

amenities include electrical, water, and sewer hookups; Wi-Fi; a dump station; and show-ers. *Located just west of the Parkway off the US 412 exit.* **GPS: N35° 34.688' W87° 25.882'**

Bike-In/Hike-In Campgrounds

Located directly adjacent to the Parkway, the following free NPS campgrounds prohibit motorized vehicles, making them perfect for a biking trip along the Trace. Call 800-305-7417 or visit nps.gov/natr for more information.

Kosciusko, MS (Milepost 160.0)

Kosciusko Bicycle-Only Campground Enter the road marked DISTRICT RANGER OFFICE just south of the Kosciusko Welcome Center. On this road, a tent symbol and arrow will direct you into the camping area, on your right. Picnic tables, tent pads, and fire grates are available; restrooms and water are available year-round outside the Welcome Center. **GPS: N33° 02.262' W89° 34.740'**

Houston, MS (Milepost 234.0)

Witch Dance Bicycle-Only Campground Camping is permitted in the picnic area adjacent to the restrooms and in the horse-staging area but is prohibited in the north picnic loop. Restrooms, picnic tables, fire grates, and drinking water are available. **GPS: N33° 54.690' W88° 56.400'**

Parkway Visitor Center, Tupelo, MS (Milepost 266.0)

Tupelo Bicycle-Only Campground Camping is available at an outdoor classroom across the road from the Parkway Visitor Center—cross the Parkway at the south end of the parking lot, proceed through all four lanes of traffic, and continue on this road to the small parking area/trailhead. Across the road from the parking area is a trail through the forest; follow this trail to the camping area. Primitive cabins, fire rings, picnic tables, grills, water, and pit toilets are available. **GPS: N34° 19.839' W88° 42.704'**

Cherokee, AL (Milepost 327.0)

Colbert Ferry Bicycle-Only Campground Enter Colbert Ferry Park, turn left, and follow the road to the left of the contact station, past the parking lot. Continue to the gated road marked with tent and bicycle symbols; then proceed through the gate and down the path to the right. Tent sites, picnic tables, grills, and fire rings are available; water and restrooms are located at the contact station. **GPS: N34° 49.990'W87° 57.013'**

Columbia, TN (Milepost 408.0)

Tennessee Highway 50 Bicycle-Only Campground Follow the signs to the TN 50 trail-head of the Natchez Trace National Scenic Trail, which is also a horse-staging area. Picnic tables, fire grates, and garbage cans are available; the nearest restrooms and water are at the Gordon House and Ferry Site, just south of TN 50. **GPS: N35° 43.303' W87° 15.757'**

INDEX

Abbreviation *MP* indicates the milepost number as described in "How to Use This Guide" (page 7) and the "How to Use the Mileposts" section (page 30). Mileposts are numbered from south to north, starting at MP 0.0 at the southern terminus at Natchez and proceeding to MP 444.0 at the northern terminus at Nashville.

A

Accessibility, wheelchair/disabilities, 57
Administrative History of the Natchez Trace Parkway (Mohlhenrich), 2
Alabama
bicycle, trails and rental, 48–50
campgrounds, 147
firearms restrictions, 31
MP on way to Tennessee, 109–15
Tennessee State Line, 117
Trace commemorative markers, 6
travel and tourism information, 138
See also Mileposts 313.0–341.8
American Indians
about Trace origins and history, 5, 14, 17–19
association with Mississippi River, 71
Cherokee Indians, 19, 71, 126, 132
Cherokee Trail of Tears, 85, 115
Chickasaw Nation, 5, 16, 18, 20–21, 23, 60–63, 76, 85, 95, 100, 110–11, 114–15, 123–24, 128–29, 138
Choctaw Nation, 19–20, 60–62, 63, 71, 76, 85–86, 88, 91, 95, 100, 114, 126, 138
Creek War of 1813-14, 127
European intrusion and destruction, 75–76
Jackson and treatment of, 114, 126
land cession and treaties, 16, 19, 62, 63, 85, 91, 95, 114, 123–24
Muscogee (Creek) Indians, 19, 71, 111, 124
Natchez Nation, 18–19, 60, 71, 73–74, 138
Seminole Indians, 19, 98, 126
tribal Nation travel and tourism information, 138
American Indian and Archaeological sites
about the category, 17–21
Grand Village of the Natchez Nation, vi, 11, 18–19, 73–74, 77
MP 10.3 Emerald Mound, 18–19, 76–77
MP 45.7 Grindstone Ford and Mangum Mound, 83
MP 61.0 Lower Choctaw Boundary, 86
MP 100.7 Choctaw Agency, 87
MP 106.9 Boyd Site, 89
MP 128.4 Upper Choctaw Boundary, 91
MP 140.0 Red Dog Road, 91
MP 176.3 Bethel Mission, 93–94
MP 213.3 Line Creek, 97
MP 232.4 Bynum Bounds, 97
MP 241.4 Chickasaw Agency, 98
MP 245.6 Monroe Mission Station, 99
MP 251.1 Chickasaw Council House, 99
MP 261.8 Chickasaw Village Site, 102–03
MP 263.9 Old Town Overlook, 103
MP 286.7 Pharr Mounds, 106–07
MP 304.5 Tishomingo State Park, 108
MP 308.4 Cave Spring, 108

MP 308.8 Bear Creek Mound, 108–09
MP 320.3 Buzzard Roost Spring, 110–11
American Revolution, 61, 95, 132

B

Baker Bluff Overlook, 25, 126
Ballard Creek, 24, 96
Battle of Ackia, 99–100
Battle of Brices Cross Roads, 22, 54, 104–05
Battle of Franklin, 64
Battle of Nashville, 64, 132
Battle of New Orleans, 5, 21, 63, 114, 126. *See also* War of 1812
Battle of Port Gibson, 22
Battle of Raymond, 21–22, 81, 86–87, 124
Battle of Shiloh, 21–22
Battle of Tupelo (aka Battle of Harrisburg), 22, 64, 100, 102
Bay Springs Lake, 24, 108
Bear Creek, 24, 44, 55, 56, 109
Bear Creek Mound, viii, 12, 18, 108–09
Bethel Mission, 20, 93–94
Bicentennial Capital Mall State Park, 7, 130
Bicycling
about Trace trails, 48–49
campgrounds, 148
shops for rental/repair, 50–51
Birdsong Hollow, 13, 26, 65, 131
Black Belt Overlook, 24, 99
Boating, rental/launches, 12, 42, 44, 57, 89, 108, 111, 147. *See also* Canoeing and kayaking
Boatman's Trail, 5
Boyd Site, 18, 89
Brices Cross Roads National Battlefield, 22, 54, 104–05
Browns Bottom, 24, 106
Bullen Creek, 24, 80
Burns Branch, 25, 128
Buzzard Roost Spring, 21, 24, 110–11
Bynum Bounds, 18, 97

C

Camping/campgrounds
adjacent National Park Service, 39–41
at nearby State Parks, 41–45
Alabama, 147
Bike-in/Hike-in, 51, 148
Mississippi, 144–47
Tennessee, 147–48
Canoeing and kayaking, 45, 56. *See also* Boating
Cave Spring, 18, 108
Cherokee, AL, vi, 147, 148
Cherokee Trail of Tears, 85, 115
Chickasaw Agency, 21, 98

TIM W. JACKSON began his publishing career at age 17, when he started covering sports for his hometown newspaper, the *Franklin County Times,* in Russellville, Alabama. He went on to earn a degree in journalism from The University of Alabama, where he worked as assistant sports editor for *The Crimson White,* the student newspaper. Since then he's worked as an editor at *Southern Living, Cooking Light,* and *Canoe & Kayak* magazines; as student-publications director at Radford University in Virginia; and as senior acquisitions editor at AdventureKEEN, Menasha Ridge Press's parent company.

Tim writes about popular culture, music, food, lifestyles, the outdoors, sports, and other topics for online and print publications including DittyTV .com, *Lost Magazine, WNC Magazine, The Asheville Post,* and *The Laurel of Asheville.* He is also the author of *Gone Pro North Carolina: Tar Heel Stars Who Became Pros* (Clerisy Press).

Based in Tuscumbia, Alabama, Tim enjoys watching sports, playing and listening to music, and spending time with his family: wife Taryn, daughter Anna, dogs Holly and Timber, and rabbit Kiwi. For more about Tim, visit timwhowritesfromhome.com.

TARYN CHASE JACKSON writes grant proposals for non-profits and has also worked for universities, museums, and educational-technology firms. Her writing has been published in *Southern Living, The Roanoke Times, The Laurel of Asheville,* the *New River Voice, Chautauquan Daily,* and *Guide to Phone Apps* magazine. Taryn has also taught workshops on memoir writing and social media for small businesses. She enjoys singing with the Shoals Chamber Singers, making mixed-media art, and shopping at estate sales. For more about Taryn, visit tarynchasejackson.com.

Tim and Taryn met at Goucher College, where they both earned MFAs in creative nonfiction. This is their second cowriting effort; their first, *Images of America: Weaverville,* a pictorial history of a North Carolina town near Asheville, was released by Arcadia Publishing in September 2015.

Check out this great title from
— Menasha Ridge Press! —

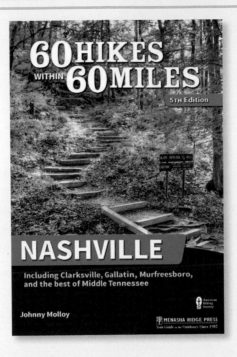

60 Hikes Within 60 Miles: Nashville

by Johnny Molloy
ISBN: 978-1-63404-340-3
$22.95, 5th Edition

6 x 9, paperback
Full color, 296 pages
Maps, photographs, index

Get outdoors with veteran Tennessee outdoors writer Johnny Molloy as he helps you find and enjoy the top hikes within 60 miles of Music City. These selected trails transport you to scenic overlooks, wildlife hot spots, and historical settings that renew your spirit and recharge your body. Take in the wildflowers and the wildlife on the Laurel Woods Trail at Beaman Park. Immerse yourself in history along the Gordon House and Ferry Site Walk.

Enjoy a hike with the entire family on the Winding Stairs. Challenge yourself with climbs and descents along the Bearwaller Gap Hiking Trail. With Johnny as your guide, you'll learn about the area and experience nature through 60 spectacular outings!

  **MENASHA RIDGE PRESS**
www.menasharidge.com

The Story of Ad

We are an independent nature a
Our founding dates back more
and now by our love of being
water, by our passion for readi
sense of wonder and discovery
time recreating outdoors in beau

It is our mission to share that wonc
especially with those who have
physical and mental health benet
activity can bring.

In addition, we strive to teach ab
so that the natural resources and
rely upon will be available for futu

We are a small team deeply roote
live and work. We have been sha
of origin—primarily Birmingham, A
and the northern suburbs of N
Drawing on the decades of experi
awareness of the industry, the ma
at large, we have shaped a unique
company that serves our readers a

We hope to meet you out on

#bewellbeoutd

"Should we stop here?" To help yo into the following categories liste

KAINTUCK BOATMEN AND THE POS

ARCHAEOLOGY AND AMERICAN IN

Prehistoric Sites

The Natchez

The Choctaw

The Chickasaw

* Indicates that the point of interest is located before the official start of the